THE BRIDPOR

POETRY AND SHOR

JUDGES
Jackie Kay • Poetry
Ali Smith • Short stories

redcliffe

First published in 2009 by Redcliffe Press Ltd
81g Pembroke Road, Bristol BS8 3EA

e: info@redcliffepress.co.uk
www.redcliffepress.co.uk

ISBN 978-1-906593-49-0

British Library Cataloguing-in-Publication Data
A catalogue record for this book is available from the British Library

Typeset by Harper Phototypesetters Ltd, Northampton
and printed by MPG Books, Bodmin

Contents

Short Story Report Ali Smith   5
Poetry Report Jackie Kay   7

Something Jenny Clarkson   8
Some Nice Stories, And One Not Natasha Soobramanien   13
The Queens From Houston N Nye   22
All of These Things Are True and Not True Joanna Quinn   33
Hollie's Dream of Consciousness Bobbie Allen   44
The Betsy Cheryl Alu   52
On Creation Anna Britten   62
Non-Invasive Dore Kiesselbach   69
By Tompion and Banger Nick MacKinnon   70
Night Drive Lydia Fulleylove   72
Iron Gall Ink Josephine Abbott   73
No Place Liz Bassett   74
Crimson Alan Buckley   76
negative space Rhonda Collis   77
Mourning Clare Diprose   78
Relationship Ben Holden   79
Fictions Rhiannon Hooson   80
Ultrasonic Mouse Deterrent Christopher Horton   81
Morning After Helen Oswald   82
Hangover Vidyan Ravinthiran   83
The Malamute Zach Falcon   84
The War Baby Helen Geoghegan   94
Don't Say Anything Kate Hendry   102
Happy Birthday Nicholas Hogg   111
I Forgot My Programme So I Went To Get It Back Joshua Lobb   121
Siren Annemarie Neary   127
In a seaside café Teresa Stenson   139

Biographies   144

ALI SMITH

Short Story Report

The short story is a powerful form, a tough and generous one. In its brief breathing space it fuses the lyric concentration of the poem and the social heft, the worldly revelation of the novel. Its formal elasticity is daunting. This is the most forgiving and simultaneously unforgiving of the literary forms. It will hugely reward a writer's courage in the handling of its structural potential and versatility, and a writer's discipline in its fundamental demand for tightness of edit and focus. It will shoulder-shruggingly deny this reward to anyone who puts a foot wrong in the composition.

This year's Bridport Prize attracted many thousands of entries in the short story category, so many that I could not possibly read them all. I received a shortlist selected by a team of experienced readers. I feel bad about not having seen the others – I wonder about every single one of them – but I profoundly trust the Bridport sifters, because what I discovered over the weeks it took me to read my knee-high box of stories was that pretty much every one they sent me was of a standard for worthy inclusion in this book. My job, therefore – to choose only a small percentage of these – wasn't at all easy. I am mourning several others that can't be included here.

What were these stories about, on the whole, and how did their writers meet their needs? Not many asked much of the form when it came to structure; not many were brave enough to be, well, slight: to trust the sleight-of-hand, the seismic shift between smallness and allness, which the story form can harness with such energy. A fair few were about marital break-up and gender anger. An awful lot were about death, or dying, or hospitals. This isn't surprising: it's a matter of life and death, after all, the short story. Its nature concerns itself with the shortness of things; by its very brevity it challenges aliveness with the certainty of mortality, and vice versa too, which is why I got very excited when I read anything which leaned towards the story form as a force and source of life. I wish there had been more of these.

In fact, I'd say this is the thing with which many of the shortlisted writers had most difficulty: the sense of an ending. Perhaps this is partly

5

because a short story's end isn't an end at all, but always a kind of beginning: the point where the story, having closed, opens for and in a reader like a germinating seed cracks open in the ground. For this reason, the point where things end must be precise – as everything in a good story must be; too many of these shortlisted stories seemed to lose their hard-won precision just when it came to the close. All good writing is about this economy, edit, rhythm and precision; the short story form demonstrates this to the other literary forms. An end, when it comes, should always send you back to the beginning, because a good story, like any real art, demands revisitation. A good short story is lifelong.

Here are some stories which still had me after I'd finished reading them, whose voices I can still hear now, whose handling of detail had implication and whose handling of their own completeness was most persuasive, all of which means they repaid the revisit, for me, and I hope for you too when you read this collection.

I've awarded the top prize to '**Something**', which of all the shortlisted pieces was the one which, for me, in its seeming partialness, most understood completeness, and which most trusted, with what looks like casualness but what is really a close-focus exactness, both precision and momentariness. Its throwaway nature is serious about what throwaway means; its breadth of social vision, in just over a thousand words, is world wide. It's really something; and it redefines the notion of the word 'something': in the beginning the word suggests lost or missed meaning and in the end its reader is left with hands full of a very definite something, both hopeless and hopeful, perfectly done.

The runners-up, '**Some Nice Stories, And One Not**', and '**The Queens from Houston**', are for me good working examples of the form's huge potential. 'The Queens from Houston' is a complete world, whose earthiness is skilfully both imagined and imaginative. 'Some Nice Stories, And One Not' is another world-opener and eye-opener, a rhythmically impressive story of impossible identities, delivered with a great deal of originality and flair in a voice whose strength is its held idiosyncracy.

JACKIE KAY

Poetry Report

I was delighted to read the entries and the choice was difficult to make. There were wonderful poems in this year's entry, so various and so commendable in many ways. In the end, I chose poems which were memorable, and touched me, poems about the age-old, time-worn themes of love and loss, relationships and grief, time and change. Poems on those themes were entered this year, again and again.

The poems that I've picked stood out because of their originality in point of view or language, or image. I was looking for something different, something that stayed with me, a different kind of clock to tell the time. I hope that everyone will enjoy this selection, various as it is, and find in each poem, an offering of something whether that be of consolation, recognition or surprise.

It was a pleasure to read them. And a great responsibility. I read all my favourite poems aloud to see how they lived off the page, and each of my choices make a good sound read as well as a paper one, the test of a good poem.

I was startled by the standard.

JENNY CLARKSON

Something

Shane Jackson couldn't hear what Ann McDonald was saying but he could read her gestures which said 'here is the something area', 'this is the person who something', 'over there is the something'. He didn't have his iPod turned on so he was making words happen in his head, supported by the complex beat of potatoes rumbling along the conveyor.

'It's important not to something,' said Ann McDonald's arms and expression.

'Hit-the-beat, hit-on-the-beat, hit-on-the-beat-beat,' Shane chanted to himself, walking in time and tapping his fingers on his thighs inside his pockets.

A line of people were grabbing off certain potatoes as they went by at top speed.

'Got it,' thought Shane. 'Got-it-bro, got-the-beat, got-the-word, got-it-got-it-bro.'

He saw Darren Headland in the line, dressed in a shapeless navy blue coat and matching cap, wearing giant headphones. He leered at him behind Ann McDonald's back.

'Where do you live?' asked Ann McDonald as they headed back to the office. Her words sounded as if they were wrapped in cotton wool.

'Harrison Road.' His voice was wrapped in it too. 'My voice sounds weird,' he told her.

'Don't worry, you'll be issued with ear protectors.'

They sat down on either side of Ann McDonald's desk. Ann McDonald wrote Harrison Road then underlined it. Shane looked at a scuff on his new trainers then licked a finger and rubbed at it. It was only dust.

'What made you want to work at Harlequin Potatoes?'

'My mum,' said Shane.

In the background the potatoes sounded like a non-stop landslide.

'Have you worked anywhere before, Shane?' asked Ann McDonald.

'Not legally,' said Shane.

Ann McDonald looked at the sheet of paper in front of her. Shane looked around, at a giant poster with the slogan 'Harlequin Potatoes: Quality Assured', at the year planner filled in with blue and green and red felt tips, at the framed certificates with 'Ann McDonald' in bold black type and smaller writing which he couldn't read.

'Would I have to wear the jacket and the hat, Miss?'

'Yes. Do you have a problem with that?'

Shane half laughed, half snorted.

Ann McDonald's mobile phone started to vibrate.

'Would you excuse me a moment, Shane?' She said.

The rumbling from the factory floor increased then decreased as she opened the door, went out, closed it again.

'No something something,' Shane heard her say. 'Something can't something something unreasonable something something something not possible something something absolutely enough something something.'

Shane got up from his chair and looked out of the window. A long way off, in the corner of the site, was a hill made of potatoes. A red tractor was pulling a trailer loaded with more potatoes towards it. He could hear music coming from the cab.

When Ann McDonald returned, breathing as if she had been walking fast, Shane was sitting with his earphones in. He took them out and asked, 'Everything alright, Miss?'

'Fine, thank you,' said Ann McDonald, putting her phone in her top drawer. 'Now, Shane, if I give you this job, are you prepared to work hard, come in on time, do what you are told?'

Shane said nothing for quite a long time. Just as Ann McDonald took in a breath, ready to speak again, he answered.

'Well, Miss. What I think is, this job doesn't look like much fun. But I would really like the money. I'm not very good at getting up early. I stay up quite late, you know. I don't like being told what to do. I had enough of that at school. I'll tell you this. Show me how to do something once and I've got it. One thing is, I couldn't be without my music. What I'm thinking is, I could put in my earphones under those ear protector things. Sorted. I know you find it hard to get people to work here. Otherwise you wouldn't be asking me along, would you? What I say is, you play ball with me, I'll play ball with you.'

'Have you quite finished?' asked Ann McDonald.

'Oh, yes, and would I get to drive the tractor?' He grinned.

'Have you driven a tractor before?'

'Not legally.'

A rumbling started in Ann McDonald's top drawer.

'Sorry, Shane,' said Ann McDonald, getting up from her desk.

She opened the door. The rumbling from the factory filled the room. She closed the door and it returned to the factory.

Shane walked round to Ann McDonald's side of the desk, looked at his name, his address. Underneath was written a long word which he couldn't read and the word 'chatty' with an exclamation mark after it. From outside he could hear Ann McDonald occasionally raise her voice to say words like 'no', 'never' and 'enough'.

Back at her desk, Ann McDonald put her phone back in the drawer. Her hand was shaking slightly. Her neck had come out in red blotches.

'I'd switch it off if I were you.'

She ignored him, either reading or pretending to read the paper in front of her.

She looked up. 'We can take you on for 16 hours a week, at £4.77 an hour, starting tomorrow at 8 am.'

'Cool,' said Shane.

'You can go now.'

Shane stayed sitting in his chair. Ann McDonald looked at the door.

'Can I say something, Miss?'

'Yes, but I've got an appointment very shortly.'

'My mum used to get calls like that. In the end, her mate said call in the police. She didn't want to. Obviously. They don't take much notice of our family, if you know what I mean. But she was nearly cracking up. So she did. She got a restraining order. It's not just for not going near someone. It can be for not phoning them too. Now everything's OK. I just wanted to tell you that, Miss.'

'Thank you, Shane. I can assure you there's nothing to worry about.'

They walked from either side of the desk and met at the door. As Ann McDonald's hand reached the door handle, her drawer started to rumble again. Shane ran, leaped over the desk, took out the phone and switched it off. He handed it to her proudly.

'You really shouldn't have done that, Shane. The jumping over my desk, the turning my phone off.'

'Have you got protection?' Shane said very quietly.

'Pardon?' said Ann McDonald.

'Protection, Miss.'

Ann McDonald's eyes widened.

'Just in case, Miss. Not that you're ever going to use it. Just in case someone was to come at you.' His hand was automatically at the back of his jeans waistband.

Ann McDonald took two steps backwards.

'If you're talking about what I think you're talking about,' she said, 'it is a very foolish thing to do. It won't protect you. An attacker will grab it off you and use it himself. You put yourself in more danger.'

'That's what they want you to believe. But they're wrong and they know they're wrong. Go and ask the people in there. They'll tell you. It's part of life. What I think is, you are a nice lady, like my mum is,' he put his arm round Ann McDonald's shoulders, 'I don't want you to be upset. You need to get more tough.'

He released her and walked off down the corridor in his half-dancing way, turned back and called, 'See you tomorrow, Miss' but the door had already closed.

As he passed the window, he saw Ann McDonald take a mirror from her handbag, look at her face, slide red lipstick over her lips.

He sat down near the exit gate on a concrete slab, surrounded by silent fields of potatoes. Every so often, he looked towards the door he thought Darren Headland would appear from. The smell of rotting from the hill in the distance was all around him and inside him. He had his earphones in. He was thinking about a girl he had seen on the bus.

NATASHA SOOBRAMANIEN

Some Nice Stories, And One Not

I

Nana Sanderson or Neisha Suleiman or Nikita Schulz or Norma Strang stands on Boulevard Rothschild in central Tel Aviv on a warm, late-spring afternoon, trying to take a photo of three friends who have walked on ahead of her under a bower of flowering trees shedding lilac petals which, crushed underfoot, look greasy rather than papery, as they might have done had they really resembled the confetti to which she would like to liken them.

But they keep moving. The friends, not the petals, which do not move as there is no wind and anyway, they are too gummy. They stick to the ground like wet confetti. And neither do the flowering trees appear to move, but move they must on occasion, or shiver, at least, as shown by the mess of lilac petals on the ground. Flowering trees are an extravagance, Nuala feels. They are unnecessary. Unnatural. Showy. Inappropriate. Don't they know what's going on here? It's hard to focus but she uses the trees to frame the fast diminishing figures of her three friends who have not yet noticed that she has dropped back to take the photo. She takes the photo. She does not, in the manner of most people nowadays, choose to review the photo once she has taken it. She prefers instead to wait some time after the moment of taking a photo, long after she has left the location of the photo itself, before checking to see what she's got. Later, when she is back in the flat of Yotan and Pia, two of the friends in the photo, she will find that she has inadvertently framed it in such a way that Luca, the third friend and the one with whom she has travelled here from London, appears to be packed inside Yotan's rucksack with only his head peeping out. And later during her holiday – though she is at pains not to refer to her trip as such, how could it be, here? – she will overcome her prejudice, realising that the instant review of one's photos is how one

13

learns to improve them, not least because the moment at which one clicks is not always the moment captured: certainly her camera operates on some kind of delay, so that she has almost to be psychic, clicking just a moment before the moment she wants to record. If, for example, she wished to photograph a dog on Tel Aviv beach, a grey Great Dane with a lavender sheen, say, around whose neck hangs the kind of chain one might see on a rap star, a chain that seems to empower rather than enslave, whose fat links lie flat on his thick neck and wink as he runs, if she wished to photograph this dog in a spray of sand damp and dark like Muscovado sugar as he leaps to catch a frisbee in his mouth, she must press the button the moment the dog readies itself to jump. Otherwise, she will miss the point of the photograph. And this, the fact of having to pre-empt the moment she wishes to record, she discovers only once she has overcome her prejudice against the instant review, a discovery which occurs later on in the holiday, which is not really a holiday, and later on in this story, which is not really a story but an account of the impossibility of knowing exactly which story to tell, and the anxiety caused by this impossibility which means that in the end – for all stories must end – all one can do is tell *all* the stories which occur on this trip, not just the nice stories but the depressing stories, the pointless stories, the boring stories, the most depressing and pointless and boring of which will occur towards the end of the trip and this account of the trip, somewhere between Ramallah and Jerusalem. But right now, right at this moment, the moment after she has taken her photograph, we are still in Tel Aviv, central Tel Aviv, on a warm, late-spring afternoon on the Boulevard Rothschild.

II

In Tel Aviv, people speak to Nell in Hebrew: not hesitantly but forthrightly, confident they will be understood. This happens to Luca too. Both of them have those kinds of faces which are useful mainly in the Middle East, the Mediterranean, North Africa and Central and South America, if one wants to be taken for a local. And by extension, in that respect, theirs are not such useful faces in Scandinavia or Central or Eastern Europe. On arrival at the airport, excited to be here, they ask Yotan, who has come to meet them, if they look Israeli. Not you, he tells Niamh; only now, he tells her, away from London and under these airport lights can he finally see the Chinese in her, an observation she will remember at the Ramallah-Jerusalem border-crossing post some days later. As they leave the airport, Namora comments on the number of flags they pass, in celebration of the 60th anniversary of Israel's independence, the exact date of which she was disputing with Luca on the flight over. You are both right, says Yotan, telling them about the two calendars, Jewish and Roman. But Luca is more right than you.

Since arriving in Tel Aviv three days ago Nagmeh has walked up and down this Boulevard several times on her way to the beach or the market or the bus station. In London, a city she has lived in for most of her life and where she now shares a flat with Luca, she often gets lost. How come you can suddenly get us from A to B without taking in the rest of the alphabet, he asks her. How come you can find your way to the beach or the market or the bus station so quickly, so directly, when we have only been shown the way once? Because in this country, she tells him, I cannot walk around with my eyes closed.

Naomi has based much of her opinion of Tel Aviv and Tel Avivians on what she has observed of life on this Boulevard, which lies like a spine down the centre of the city, which makes it easier for her to navigate. She has noticed that:

Tel Avivians have nice dogs
Tel Avivian men are manly
Tel Avivian women are womanly
Tel Avivians have nice bodies
Tel Avivians like to wear sunglasses
Tel Avivians like to look at each other
Tel Avivians like to look at themselves in each other's sunglasses
Tel Avivians like to sit around in cafes and bars with their dogs
Tel Avivian bars in new buildings on the corners of streets which intersect the Boulevard are mirrored like a hit man's shades and look more like banks or offices.

But the Tel Avivians – who are probably not from Tel Aviv – to be observed around the bus station and in the parks by the bus stations and hanging around in the stretches of waste ground between the market and the beach are nothing like the Tel Avivians strolling past now as she walks down Boulevard Rothschild towards the friends who have stopped and are waiting for her. She catches them up and together they turn off the Boulevard, towards home.

III

What's wrong, she asks Luca later that evening as they lie top to toe on parallel mattresses in the spare room of Yotan and his girlfriend Pia, whom Nyeki will later refer to as *mishmish*, the word in both Hebrew and Arabic for apricot, a word Yotan will teach her and a word she will later recall on the way to the airport, shortly after the depressing and pointless and boring encounter with the heavily-armed soldier at the Ramallah-Jerusalem border-crossing post which takes place towards the end of this account.

I'm lonely, says Luca.
So am I, she replies.
And have you noticed, Luca says, How Yotan has not said anything?
About what?
About how things are here. He has not once asked us what we think. Have you noticed that?
Yes, says Nerissa.

And they both try to sleep but the window is open and the sounds of the emergency services' sirens in Tel Aviv are different to those in London.

Three days into their trip they feel as though they have not yet quite arrived. So far the trip — the country — is not as they imagined it would be. But later on, when they are back in London, and people ask about the country — their trip — they will find that they have, between them, a fund of nice stories on which to draw: stories which will illustrate some aspect of their experience here, stories which will seem to them to gesture towards some greater significance which they cannot, dare not, consider here, just yet, in this country where everything is significant, where nothing, as Yotan will point out, is casual: when, at a literary festival a day or two later, they hear a reading of a found text by a Palestinian writer which includes a passing reference to a friendly settler, Yotan will tell them that its inclusion in this story, at this event, by this writer, at this time has been deliberated on; is deliberate. One of their nice stories is also from this festival: two musicians from the Edward Said Conservatory, at the last minute, and for reasons not divulged by the authorities, are prevented from joining their colleagues to perform at the closing ceremony. The sextet, now a quartet, is obliged to play a piece for which they have not rehearsed. Every hesitation, every wrong note, is part of this story. Another is from their time at the beach in Tel Aviv: near where they lounge, a toddler (plump and brown in a turquoise swimsuit, the middle frilled), is spading sand into a bucket and conversing sociably with herself. Yotan asks her name and when she replies, he laughs.

What did she say? They ask.
Me, he says. My name is Me.

There is the far away sound of sirens and the intimate whine of mosquitoes and then, from out on the balcony, just outside their window, there are the wind chimes.

IV

Some days later, Nairoji and Luca travel on to Jerusalem. While walking around Jerusalem's narrow streets, past openly armed civilians, through the old city with its stone steps worn like soap on which she slips in her flip-flops, she looks back on her time in Tel Aviv and thinks:

Tel Avivians aren't as heavily armed
Tel Avivians are more hedonistic
Te Avivians are sexier
Tel Avivians aren't as serious and political
Tel Avivians are richer
Tel Avivians dress better
Tel Avivians are more aloof

She could add to her observations about the two cities the fact that Jerusalem is harder to navigate – no Boulevard Rothschild here – though still she negotiates the place more easily than she does London. Negotiating Jerusalem is best done without outside help, she finds, as the process is often complicated by misdirections or indirections received from well-meaning strangers: asking the way to the market prompts three different, not

17

to say conflicting, responses, including one that involves a long detour – the kind stranger points out proudly – to avoid their passing through the Arab Quarter. After similar incidents they must conclude that left and right carry a different significance here, a significance which is lost on them.

In Jerusalem, they stay in a flat owned by Yotan's aunt who lives next door. Yotan's aunt reminds Nadine of Tel Aviv. Specifically, the Bauhaus apartment buildings there. Yotan later admits that these buildings are not really Bauhaus: this being a story put about by the tourist board. She is anachronistic and European, lean and spare and good-looking in a stark way. She has clean lines. So do her opinions. These buildings are being eroded, Yotan tells her; eaten away by the salt in the coastal breezes. The flat is plain. It is kitted out with furniture and kitchenware like their furniture and their kitchenware at home. The shelves are full of books with titles such as, *The Truth about the Arabs*, or *The Secret War Against the Jews*. Yotan's aunt assumes that Noleta and Luca are together. She shows them their room. When she has left, Luca moves his bag into the other room. Later, at the end of the trip, at the airport on their way home, a security official will ask Nancy the nature of her relationship with Luca, and she will reply that he is her best friend. And when the official does not appear satisfied with this explanation, she will say, We used to be lovers but now he is my friend.

After lunch with Yotan's aunt and her friends, she takes Narcissus and Luca up to a promenade on the hill which looks out over Jerusalem. At lunch, Yotan's aunt and her friends told stories of interlopers, intruders, threats, murderous intentions, security, fear, irreconcilable differences, self-determination and identity, while Nessa and Luca ate watermelon. They stroll along paths bordered by spiky broom, the sun extreme against the whitish pink of the flagstones, and stop at a viewing terrace to look out over the city. They see the Dome of the Rock, which shimmers like a mirage even as Yotan's aunt openly wishes it away: in her flat she has on display a doctored photo of this scene, the Dome of the Rock replaced with a synagogue. She points out the Arab Quarter; where it used to end and how it has extended, its expansion now limited by the wall which has been erected at the far edge of their vision. Nascha is finding it hard to hide her anger at the assumptions Yotan's aunt has made about them, and Luca, sensing this, takes the arm of Yotan's aunt and leads her away to look at a nearby flock of birds, which are tearing at the ground. Nerys remains on the terrace, leaning on the terrace wall, watching a man beside her who sketches the view. On the wall in front of her is fixed a brass plaque, engraved with the outline of the city, and a key indicating which buildings can be seen. This is the view that the dark-haired man is sketching. She closes her eyes and traces the engraving, but she cannot distinguish between the buildings by touch alone: the engraving is too fine or her fingers are perhaps still sticky from the watermelon at lunch. As a child, she did not like watermelon. She resented the pips. But as an adult, she accepts them and removes them without complaint. She can hear Luca asking Yotan's aunt about the birds, what kind they are. She can hear Yotan's aunt reply that these birds are interlopers, scavengers, intruders, murderers that are hunting down indigenous species and killing them off. Nico, eyes still closed, continues to run her fingers along the brass plaque, ignoring the voice of Yotan's aunt, and fixing instead on the soft, regular sound of the dark-haired man's pencil. The sounds his pencil make are considered, deliberate, meaningful, like a kind of code.

V

The next day, Natalie and Luca travel to the other side of the wall. Their first border crossing of the day, through the Jerusalem-Bethlehem post, is uneventful. On the other side of the Separation wall – what else, thinks Nula, is a wall supposed to do? – they follow it a little way and note how, like a tourist, it takes detours to take in all the attractive sights nearby: an olive grove, a well. They walk into Bethlehem and from there, take a taxi to Ramallah. The driver, like all taxi drivers, tells them stories, most of which are depressing or pointless or boring so Nefertiti stops listening and looks out instead at the camo-coloured desert which looks flat and featureless and same-old-samey until with staring it comes alive: a lizard shivers into being from the sand and darts behind a rock, then suddenly the landscape springs into 3D: she sees contours and shadows and hollows and boulders and all the while they are driving on towards Ramallah, where they will stop for a while.

In Ramallah, Nneke takes photographs. It is as this point that she learns to overcome her prejudice, and reviews what she takes instantly: she does not know if she will ever return to Ramallah. She checks that the camera has recorded what she wants to record, which among other things is:

A map of Israel and the West Bank, pasted to the wall and ripped in places
A little boy who sells them some chewing gum
Graffiti in Arabic, which she doesn't understand
Carcasses of unidentifiable animals hanging in a butcher's shop
Open sacks of spices and dried flowers in the market
A sign for a coffee shop which looks like a Starbucks, but isn't

They go to a stationer's shop, where they find sheets of stickers depicting Palestinian flags. Until now, they have seen only Israeli flags on display, and some American ones. Nevada buys a few sheets of these stickers. It is not until a few days later, at the airport, undergoing a prolonged and thorough security check during which all aspects of her luggage and possessions are swabbed, that she will suddenly remember these stickers and wonder at the questions, the consequences, if these are found. It is not until then that she will wonder exactly why she bought these stickers, and what story she will tell the security officer who finds them:

I collect stickers
I collect stickers of flags of the world and am missing Palestine
My nephew collects stickers of flags of the world and is missing Palestine
My nephew has a Palestinian father
My nephew's Palestinian father left them when the son was very young.
He has never known his father. Also, he collects stickers.

But that is a few days later and right now, Nusha is in Ramallah, paying for the stickers, and thinking that they ought to find a taxi to drive them up to the Ramallah-Jerusalem border-crossing post and her encounter there with the soldier who will question her origins, will question who she is, refusing to recognise that she is from where she says she is from.

And in the end, there is nothing more to tell. Or rather, the incident is too boring, too pointless, too depressing to relate. When the soldier finally tells her she is free to leave, she remembers a recent night out in a bar on Jaffa Street with Luca, when they met a soldier just like him. He drank fig arak with them and said, The only Arabic I know is *Stop or I'll shoot*. So Noa taught him a new word, a word Yotan taught her. She remembers this now, and, as she puts her passport away, she says to the heavily-armed soldier at the Ramallah-Jerusalem border-crossing post who is so stoned his eyes are almost closed and it is *he* who now looks Chinese, *shukran*, which is Arabic for 'thank you'.

VI

As Yotan and Pia drive Noemi and Luca to the airport, to catch their flight to London, Pia tells stories of her various encounters with airport security staff on her travels to and from Israel. Pia is German. Yotan met Pia in London, when he was stopped and searched by anti-terrorist police because he fit the description of someone they were looking for. And he seemed to fit too the description of someone Pia was looking for; she saw the search and went to him after to see that he was alright and when she did, he was. Nadege thinks they are lucky to have such a nice story. Such stories are rare. Pia, who is in the passenger seat, leans round towards them in the back and invites them to take, from a brown paper bag full of them, an apricot. Then Nicole remembers *mishmish*, the word Yotan taught her, which means the same in both Hebrew and Arabic, and laughs: Pia, small and neatly-made, her shallow curves and her golden skin. Neena tells everyone her new nickname for Pia, as she reaches deep into the bag and takes one.

The stories – nice or otherwise – end when the security checks are completed and they are escorted onto the plane. Nothing much happens after this: they sleep, land, clear customs quickly, then travel from the airport into London with little incident. In the city, they hail a cab and on climbing in, are reminded that today is the day of the Champions League final between Chelsea and Manchester United: their driver is a Chelsea fan. He is wearing a Chelsea shirt and Chelsea scarf and the glass partition which separates driver from passenger is covered in Chelsea stickers. But it is pointless to recount their conversation with him, their banter about the match, which Natasha and Luca would prefer Manchester United won, being Arsenal fans and no friends of Chelsea; it is pointless to recount all this, as they are back home in London now, their arrival marking the end of this account of their trip and anyway, theirs was much like any other football banter with any other cab driver the world over and you may well have heard it all before.

N NYE

The Queens From Houston

Kathy knew it wouldn't do any good to talk nonsense to him. He was as literal as the field, the empty pasture that stretched out yearning to Kansas. She talked straight and simple to him, told him the truth, talked about what could be seen or felt between the fingers, like that clayey soil out in the field. What she had learned, married to his son Winston, named for the one-time hope of the western world.

Old Lawrence lived in the trailer they had moved onto the lot next to the house. He couldn't stay out on his farm after Sadie died and where else would he go? Winston laid it out plain, this was his dad, he couldn't put him away in the Far View Home over in Simla, and he knew, what with the four kids, there was no way to put him up in the house.

So Win got the trailer cheap from Ed Hoskins who used to take it up hunting in the mountains in the fall during deer season. Lawrence and Win went along year after year, bringing home buck, since Kathy wouldn't have the does, wouldn't roast a venison doe with potatoes and carrots and onions simmered in the juice. Said she didn't care if the bucks were tougher, that's the way it was. They froze the buck in roasts and ground, some chops, and ate it off and on all winter.

Old Lawrence said he could tell when Kathy had taken out a bundle from the freezer, could smell it before it even started to sizzle. Went out and picked her something to let her know he was glad. Did the same for the honey she pulled from her bee hives, so thick and sweet on his tongue, he dreamed about it nights. Picked her a bunch of dried barrel thistle, a clutch of misty green sage that crumbled pungent in his hands, bringing it in to her. There at the stove, her cheeks red as apples, he'd pinch one, and she let him get away with it. Sent him packing after, though.

Kathy was relieved he stuck to pinching her cheeks and not her bum. He ever started doing that, she'd have to talk to Win. As it was, she knew Old Lawrence liked her, didn't just put up with her, and it was just the two of them all day around the place, the kids at school and Win in town at the Ford shop, fixing cars.

God, she was glad she had a man could do something useful like keep the truck running. Worth his weight, worth the things she didn't like as well, some heavy drinking, and like his dad, a flair with women. She didn't think Win had run around on her yet, but the possibility hung out there like the sheets on the line flapping in the wind.

Nice smell of sun in the sheets drying outside. She pinned Win's shirts on the next line, and the kids' jeans, even though the kids complained the jeans were too stiff when she dried them outside. She didn't care today what they thought, she meant to spend her time outdoors, let the wind mess with her hair, feel the caress of the gusts, her own little extra-marital affair.

Lawrence came out of his trailer and waved as he walked past, headed for his car parked off to the side of the back lot, a nice blue '67 Chevy Kathy wouldn't mind having for her own.

'Where you headed today, Lawrence?' she called.

'Out to Kansas,' he yelled back, the wind taking his words in the right direction. 'Be back for dinner or send the State Patrol.'

Kathy checked her watch. Ten-thirty a.m. When he said dinner, he meant the noon meal. Kansas was a good seventy-five miles east, not likely he'd make it. But then he really wasn't going to Kansas, or anywhere close. Car hadn't run in a couple of years.

'Son, you need to check the battery on the Chevy, it don't start too good,' Lawrence complained on the average of once a week.

'I'll look at it this weekend,' Win said, and sometimes he did, even charging it up with the truck so the lights would work if Lawrence went for a night drive, and just so the blinkers would come on when he signalled a turn.

No matter how good the battery still was, the gas tank was empty, the right rear axle sat on a cement block instead of a tire, and bumper high weeds had grown up around the Chevy, stranding it except for a narrow path that led to the driver's side.

Kathy waved as Lawrence slammed the car door and turned the ignition. The usual grinding, as the engine sucked for gas, then Lawrence was on his way, signaling his right turn onto the highway, headed east.

Kathy turned back to the clothes line and hung up the rest of the clothes. She'd work in the garden next, pull up the last of the carrots, tear down the snap bean vines, keep her eye on Lawrence on his way to Kansas. Let the wind have its way with her.

Lawrence was proud how the car still handled on the open stretches. He liked heading east where the road lost itself mile after mile, flat out, nothing to disturb the view, and not much traffic. Course he had an early start on the holiday folks.

Going over to see Houston Islay, not what you think, not some other rancher with a herd. No, Houston was a lady friend Lawrence had kept company with ever since Sadie passed on. Well, truth tell, even before then, Lawrence confessed to the Chevy, which knew better anyway, Houston having sat herself right in the front seat on more than one occasion. Had him drive her to Abilene once. Her from Russell Springs, not much of a place, runs an antique store there. How's he met her, there in her china shop.

'Can I help you?' He can hear her say it even now, years past.

Nice plump lady, hair done up fancy in a roll at the back of her head with a bunch of pins he loves to have her remove for him. Wearing a load of sweaters and shawls since it's cold in the shop, and he can't get an eye for her frame besides the plump.

'Looking for old farm implements, old tools, wooden handles, iron blades, you know what I mean,' he'd told her, sizing her up.

'Hmm,' she considered, looking around at the predominance of glassware, blinking in the sun, the china displayed for all the world like new, even with its cracks and chips. Pure character she tells him later, like a body's been around. Hers with its stretch marks, loose flesh on her upper arms he likes to tickle in his puckered lips. Can't believe at his age, at hers, they can find such glory on that scratchy horsehair sofa she has in the back, after she hangs out the Be Back Tomorrow sign on the door. It still swinging when she takes the first pins out of all that hair. Him nearly bald even then.

But first they negotiated over some rakes and hoes she had in a shed nearby, and he took her over to the Bluebird Café for some lunch, and she laughed deep and long, and he fell for her, hadn't meant to, had only meant to drive some back roads looking for old stuff, the fields fallow that time of year, Sadie busy with some ladies from church. He didn't have anything to do, and drove east. Been doing it years since, nobody but him and Houston knew a thing about it. Their secret, fine with both of them, her already a widow, happy for a little tumble now and then, and him too, thought those days were over. Glad he was wrong.

Back at the shop, she closed up, hung that sign. He lost count of the days he watched that sign swing behind her as she took off the layers of sweaters, down to her buff, and then him too, and they had a go of it on the maroon sofa, beautiful colour against her white skin, her long thick hair he watched turn white over the years, while his fell out but for a fringe. Just thinking about her made the miles fly.

He didn't mind the drive, got him out of the house, gave him something to do. He had quite a collection of hoes and rakes, brought home an old hayrack one time. Had to rent a trailer for that, then pull the trailer back on a quick round trip. Surprised Houston at night in her own bed piled with pillows of all sizes, satin sheets he nearly slid out of onto the floor, and she laughed. God, she could laugh, right out of her lungs she would laugh at him and pull him to her. Some good old times they had.

He stopped at the crossroads of U.S. 40 and 385, running north and south. No cars. Pulled forward, still heading east.

Kathy finished up in the garden, and by then the sheets had blown dry, full of the smell of the field, dried tumbleweed, thistle, earth. Lawrence was intent on his driving, both hands on the wheel, staring straight ahead, a cautious driver, she didn't have to worry. Thought she'd hike off to the grove, check her hives, before she came back to make him his dinner, some soup and fresh bread and the honey he loved. Some days they ate together at the table in the kitchen, him telling her stories. Other times, he took his food over to the trailer to watch TV while he ate. She wouldn't let him turn on the tube in her house during the day.

'I'll just get caught up in it,' she told him.

'That's the idea, missy,' he told her back. 'Get you hooked.'

She shook her head. 'Those shows only give you bits and pieces of the story, so I have to watch every day to keep track of what's going on, who's who. I don't want the hassle.'

Wind keeps me stirred up, she might have told him, but didn't want to get personal.

What Lawrence liked about the soaps was how they were closer to real life than anyone really knew, unless you were living the life yourself, as he imagined a lot of folks were but not letting on. What with Houston over the line in Kansas, his life had taken a turn in that direction, toward secrecy and little lies that piled up into whole seasons, and then years. While Sadie got cancer, and went into remission, and the boys married and had their own kids, and Sadie got sick again. And then Will got divorced after Polly ran around and got caught, and Will signed up on a

Merchant Marine ship, of all things, his own son, a hardscrabble boy, sending home postcards from Peru, the United Emirates, God knows. He was off Japan when Sadie finally kicked in for good. Never made it home in time for the funeral and would probably feel bad about it the rest of his life, her favourite of all the boys.

The thing was, Houston understood all this, listened to him tell it all, asked questions when he showed up, which was real irregular, especially towards the last with Sadie. Didn't want to leave her alone in the hospital. Brought her home for the last week, like she asked, and set her up on a rented crank-up bed right there in the parlour, with a view out toward the barn and her truck garden gone to seed.

'How's Sadie's treatments going? How're the boys? Where's Will these days?' Houston asked, like she really cared, and Lawrence thought she did. Knew what mattered to him and didn't expect to have him to herself.

Time came when he drove over to Russell Springs, Kansas, a widower. Made him think of a winnower, the chaff blowing off into the wind, the way he flew east to Houston, leaving the husk of himself back on the empty farm.

'It's over,' he told her right off.

She misunderstood. Thought he wasn't coming back, had to call it quits due to Sadie.

'No, no,' he explained to her startled eyes, violet they were, under heavy lids he had kissed as she slept, and then left her to drive back across the open country in the middle of the night, too many times to remember.

'Sadie's gone. And buried,' he said. 'The boys, all but Will, carried her out to the plot. Couldn't locate Will until too late.'

Houston took him into herself, took the chaff and caught it from flying away, held him for so long, he started to feel smothered before she let him go. Knew she meant to comfort him. Then she made tea on the little hot plate she had in the shop. Took two cups right from the glass display case, two special ones wreathed with roses looked like. Too fragile for his big knobby hands, but she said nonsense and dropped in two perfect cubes of sugar. Stirred it with a little silver spoon said Montreal on the end.

'Came from the World's Fair in '67,' she told him. 'Some folks try to collect every one from a World's Fair.'

The tea was hot and scalded his throat going down, so she cooled it off with a little whisky she had, what she usually gave him.

'You know we could marry now,' he told her violet eyes, the layers of shawls and sweaters he knew what hid, her cheeks rosy from the hot tea.

She looked back hard at him but smiling. 'Could, I guess,' she said and took a sip from that delicate cup. 'But won't.'

'Too old?' he asked her, wondering why she wouldn't have him after all this time.

She laughed her good big laugh that set her flesh moving. 'I don't know that now is the time to be deciding. You need to live a while with Sadie gone, see how you feel.'

'But say we think about it,' he answered. 'I'd like you to meet the boys, see the farm, come on back with me to Colorado. Save the drive.'

'Oh, you love that drive, Lawrence. Love coming out to Kansas to see me. All of that would change with me underfoot, in Sadie's kitchen, in your marriage bed.'

He couldn't imagine her in his house, he had to admit. Couldn't see her things there, the teacups, the fringed shawls, the satin sheets, her dozen cats with names of famous women, Eleanor, Bathsheba, Cleo, Willa, St. Agnes, oh he could never keep them straight.

'How's it you're so smart?' he teased her, and they laughed long and hard, with a little more whisky than tea as the dusk fell, imagining how they'd explain themselves to anyone, his boys, his neighbours, the pastor at his church.

'And what do they think of you here in Russell Springs with a regular customer who gets you to close the shop every time he comes to buy?'

She pulled her shawl up to her nose, tossed its fringed end over her shoulder and squinted the violet eyes. 'I'm the Mystery Woman to them, and who doesn't love a good mystery? Oh, I know they talk, but I ignore it. Go to church on Sunday, used to sing in the choir, attend a social now and then. Eat out at all the cafés on a rotating basis. Pick no favourites, keep them guessing.

'I have friends, we play cribbage or canasta, gossip. They've asked about you, and I tell them you're a good friend from way back. As you are, are you not?'

'The best,' he told her, in love with her all over again, all fresh and flushed with it and the whisky. She was right. Had a good thing going without getting hitched. Also thought she had no intention of leaving her shop and house, Russell Springs.

Time was he'd go over pretty regular, once a week, and stay for a day or two. That's when she had him take her to Abilene, and another time Dodge City, looking for one thing or another for a customer. Got so she'd even have dinner ready he was so predictable, and he enjoyed walking in on a home-cooked meal and the smells, even when she'd try something foreign on him. He was hoping today she'd have baked a cake. In the mood for sweets lately, couldn't get his fill.

Out in the grove, the white hives stood on platforms scattered under mixed scrub oak, piñon, and a couple of tall cottonwoods. Some farm woman had planted the trees long ago, wind had done the pruning. The trunks twisted and bent, the branches and limbs reached out in greeting like friendly neighbours, but a lot less trouble. On the far side, a thin creek ran with water in the spring and after a downpour. Today, Kathy knew it would be as dry as the leaves still left on the trees, shrivelled, brown, and dusty.

She had built the hives from plans she got at the county extension. Got the wood and had Win cut it, nailed the boxes together and built the screens for the combs. The idea for the bees came from old Nettie English who kept bees and made honey until she died about five years ago. She sat out on the road under a tattered black umbrella to sell the honey each fall, just Nettie and a pyramid of shining gold jars until they were all sold. A matter of days, even hours if Nettie picked a weekend to sit out there.

'The bees will set you free,' she told Kathy. Nettie didn't care to elaborate. She just handed Kathy a small wire bail with a bit of comb and a queen and told her to get busy.

That first queen died. Kathy checked out all the books on bees and beekeeping she could get from the library over in Simla. All winter she studied and planned. Talked to Nettie who could still talk bees then but not much else. She died before she got back out to her hives that spring. Then some kids knocked them over, and the hives were lost, the bees set loose in the wind. Kathy liked to think some of them had found her grove and settled in.

What old Nettie meant by freedom was never clear. The hives were a lot of work. The honey Kathy got from the combs was like mining diamonds, but there was upkeep on the boxes, getting the hives ready for winter and cleaned again in the spring. Nettie had told her how to approach the hives to avoid stings, and usually it worked. Kathy wasn't afraid, that was the key.

'Move slowly and efficiently. Respect them. Their sweet comb is a present and never forget to thank them for their labour. Not with your mouth, with words they don't know, but with your sure hands and your heart.'

Nettie's voice was always with her, teaching, reminding. What Kathy thought Nettie had meant by freedom was simply getting out of the house. Having a reason to take off by herself when the kids were bored enough to fight with each other, when Win got stinking drunk, when she just needed air and space around her. The grove and the hives gave her this: a place.

She made sure none of the hives had toppled, bothered by animals. She pulled up a few frames to see how far along the comb had spread on the screen, how thick it was. Soon it would be time to harvest, to render the comb into honey, and bottle it up for winter. For Lawrence, she thought, since he liked it better than anyone else. The grove was alive with bees flying out, flying in, lifted by the wind. A few landed on her hands and arms but didn't stay long and didn't sting. Curious is all.

Lawrence checked his watch as he pulled into Russell Springs. No telling just where Houston might be. The shop was open only by appointment these days, Houston cutting back, she said it was time. He thought maybe business had dropped off, but no, she had appointments most weekends, people even from Kansas City came out to see what she'd rustled up, wrung out of those ranch houses and such. He gathered she had a reputation. She sure had style.

But when he drove up in front of her house, the shades were drawn. Unlikely for Houston who liked to see what she could see. Never did tell him where she got that name. Maybe even made it up, though that wasn't like her. Every time he asked, she just said born and bred, but she didn't have that Texas drawl, and anyway, who would name a baby after a town?

He sat in the car, wondering if he should try the shop, and finally he did drive on down a couple of blocks, across from the Bluebird where they'd had their first lunch and where Mel, the new cook, called Hey, Lawrence, whenever he went over for a cup of coffee if Houston was tied up with business.

The Be Back Tomorrow sign hung in the window of the door, hung still, and the shades were drawn there too. Very unusual, Lawrence thought, when she knows I'm going to be here. In all the years, maybe it was unlikely, but they had never failed to meet up. He wasn't sure what to do. Stared at the shop, thought he might as well drive back to the house and park out back by the garage and take a nap until she showed up.

Then Mel was at the window beside him, rapping on the glass. Lawrence rolled it down.

'Hey, Lawrence, saw you through the window from the café. Guess you haven't heard.'

'Heard what?' Knowing he didn't want to hear, didn't want to know, wouldn't guess. Already knew.

'She's gone. Heart attack last Sunday coming out of church. Massive. The EMT boys rushed her to Colby, working on her the whole way. She didn't make it, Lawrence. I'm sorry to be the one to tell you.'

He didn't care what Mel thought. Let the tears roll down his cheeks. Felt his own heart crumple like a fragile tea cup dashed against a wall. He started the car. Thought about ramming it into the shop and that stupid sign, Be Back Tomorrow.

'Lawrence,' Mel said, trying to keep him from driving off. 'Lawrence?' But he just dropped his head against the steering wheel and let the car idle.

Kathy looked out her kitchen window, the soup bubbling beside her in a big pot, steam rising and fragrant. She looked over at the Chevy. Lawrence was slumped over the wheel.

She threw down the dish towel and ran on out. She knew it would happen someday. He'd just up and die, and she'd be the one to find him. Damn, she wasn't ready for it.

She reached in through the open window and touched his shoulder. 'Lawrence?'

Lawrence raised his head, and Kathy wanted to cry, wished she knew a quick prayer. Settled for a mumbled, 'Thank God.'

'What's wrong, Lawrence? I've got your dinner ready. Come on now, come on inside.'

It was Kathy. Opening the car door, reaching across him to turn off the ignition, helping him out. Somehow he must have managed to drive back across the Kansas line, back across the flat open prairie land he knew so well by now, back to his son's house. Win's not Will. Will was still at sea, hadn't been home in years. Missed his mother's funeral. Hadn't been to her grave. Kathy helped him into the house, sat him at her kitchen table. The room smelled of soup and chocolate cake. She had made him a cake after all.

'Lawrence, tell me. What's wrong, why are you upset?' She put a bowl of vegetable soup in front of him, wondering if she should call Win, get someone out here to check the old man.

'She's dead,' he said and the damn tears started up again. Maybe a lifetime of tears he'd been holding on to.

'Who? Sadie? Sadie's been dead for nearly eight years now.' Don't talk nonsense to him, Kathy told herself, tell him the truth. He prides himself on the truth, at least his version of it.

He didn't answer. Kathy let him cry. Somehow, he didn't even seem to be here, as if his drive in the Chevy had actually taken him away, back to the past maybe, beyond his grip on the real anyway. She shouldn't have gone out to the grove to check the hives, shouldn't have been lured out by the wind. She should have been watching him to see when this started.

But she couldn't watch him all day and get anything done. Maybe it was time for the Far View Home. Still, she would miss him if they sent him out there. Something about his being around she liked. They were easy together, easier than she'd ever been with her own dad. Maybe it was just a little lapse, just the beginning, and there was still time.

'Lawrence, talk,' Kathy told him, 'Tell me who died. All day we move around out here, listen to the wind, the TV, whatever. We could talk more. Stay alive.'

She didn't know what she was saying, what she wanted to say. She just wanted the old man to see her, look at her, come back.

His face was wet with tears. His voice choked out, 'Houston.' At least Kathy thought that's what he said.

'What about Houston? I've never been there, but the queens in my hives came from there. Mail order. Remember when they came? You thought I'd bought a rattlesnake because of the noise?' She laughed, but Lawrence didn't pay her any notice.

'It's down on the Gulf,' she continued. 'Hot, I hear. Someone called it the 'Bathtub of the Nation.' Have you ever been there?'

'I've been there,' he answered. 'But she's not a place.'

'She?' Kathy felt as confused as Lawrence looked. She wondered what sort of time warp they were in, or on what road, or whether they were even travelling together here in the warm kitchen that smelled of cake, a hint of dish detergent on her hands when she put them to her face.

'Runs a shop. Dresses like a gypsy. Keeps the whisky on a shelf under the counter. Be Back Tomorrow. Ha!'

'Houston?' Kathy felt cautious. She had never seen Lawrence cry, seem so far away. 'Who is she?'

'My friend from way back. Dead.'

He knew where he was. In Win's kitchen with Win's wife, Kathy. They have a bunch of kids. He probably wouldn't be going out to Kansas again. Figured Win would put a stop to that once he heard.

31

No one had known her, known his Houston, and now she was gone. Had probably been gone years, and he was just getting around to losing her.

'Eat some soup now,' Kathy told him. 'Some bread and honey that you like. Then there's cake. I made it first thing this morning. Before your drive. I'm glad you made it back for dinner and for the cake, before the kids get to it after school.

'I'm sorry about Houston,' she added.

She didn't know what to make of him, of Houston, whoever she was. Whether he had imagined it all, whether Houston was just an old memory brought alive by his trip in the Chevy. She'd ask him sometime, some other lunch, when he was in the mood for stories. She liked his stories. He remembered everything, told a good story. Had lived a lot of lives, some she guessed she didn't know about.

Behind him, on the window ledge above the sink, seven jars of last year's honey held the light of the mid-day sun, thick and gold, the work of the hives out in the grove, the drones, and the six queens from Houston. She wasn't sure what it meant that her best company was an old man getting senile, a few swarms of bees, and the wind. Or why she suddenly felt happy, watching Lawrence eat, his face still wet from tears, his hand shaking a little as he raised the spoon to his lips.

Lawrence ate the hot soup, let it scald his throat, let it bring him back home. No matter what Win was bound to say, he wasn't going to stop driving. Another time, he'd drive on over to Russell Springs, and she'd be there. Not some queen bee from Texas, but his Houston, in her sweaters and shawls, ready to laugh like always. They'd talk about how they were getting on in years, the both of them, how it was good to grow old together and pay it no mind. He'd tell her about Kathy's bees, and they'd laugh, and Houston would make a little buzzing noise in his ear and tell him she was his queen *and* his honey. He could see it, he could feel her breath tickle the hairs in his ear, he knew it better'n anything.

JOANNA QUINN

All of These Things Are True and Not True

If you want to be a spy, it is important to know true facts. Facts are chunks of information. True means they are real and have evidence, like how I am real because I was born on my birthday in 1999 in London, UK, and have had a heart beating ever since. In my spy book, there are spies with white clothes to show they are good. The facts the white spies tell you are true. However, be warned! There are also spies with black clothes who are baddies. The black spies say lies to bamboozle you. It can be confusing, keeping track of the true fact chunks, so I have made a grid in my notebook of things that are true and things that are not true.

Have you ever made a grid? It is a way of putting fact chunks in boxes to keep them safe. Like tortoises that are sleeping for winter.

Be warned again! Sometimes there are white lies. White lies are not true but sound true; they fall on you in a gentle way like snow and you don't see the badness inside. There are other words that are inappropriate, which is not allowed. Like when Uncle Marcus saw Mum in her new top that shows some of her bosom, he whistled the whit-woo builder noise and said: 'How d'you like them apples?'

'Inappropriate, Marcus,' said Mum and swung her eyeballs in my direction like the silver clack-clack balls on Dad's desk in his office.

Now firstly, this was not true as her bosoms are not apples. They don't even look like apples. When she feeds milk to my baby sister, they look more like butternut squashes with raisins on the end. Secondly, it was also inappropriate, which means you can see it on the screen in your brain but you mustn't let it slip down the mouth pipe to become word noises. I had to make a new column in my grid for this type of un-true saying. I made it with my pencil and my blue ruler.

Uncle Marcus isn't even my uncle so that is also not true. He and my Auntie Jess are friends with my mum and dad, and they came with us to Camp Bestival. Camp Bestival is a festival and they put the words 'best' and 'festival' together to say it is the best festival. I don't know about that. It's the only one I have been to. I don't know if I will be going to another one.

We went in a campervan, which Uncle Marcus hired. Me, my name is Reuben Hawkins; my sister Lily, who is four and my littler sister Eden, who isn't one yet, plus Mum, Dad, Uncle Marcus, Auntie Jess and their daughter Ava-Grace, who is twelve and at big school. A lot of people for one campervan you might think, but there is actually plenty of room because it is Space E Us. That means there is space for all of us.

'Music, Marcus! Get this party started!' said Auntie Jess, clapping her hands, as we set off in the campervan for Camp Bestival, which is by the sea.

ReginaSpektormusicReginaSpektormusic, I said in my invisible voice, which is when I say things without making a noise. Like invisible ink, which you can make with lemons, but invisible words. I would give Regina a ten out of ten.

'As long as it's not Regina bloody Spektor,' said Dad. He doesn't like her, but I do because her voice is bendy and sometimes it gets away from her like mine does in choir.

'But she is *so good,*' said Auntie Jess.

'I know!' said Mum, who was wearing her inappropriate apples top and had her sunglasses on top of her head like her hair wanted to look at the sky.

'We're having Radiohead,' said Dad.

'Remember how you always hated the music your parents played – we're going to make this lot hate Radiohead,' said Auntie Jess.

'Elkie Brooks!' shouted Mum. 'That Irish comedian does that thing about how your parents were always playing Elkie Brooks! I wept with laughter. Literally!'

Mum shouted a lot when we went to the Bestival. It's something she does when she wants you to make a face that says you are having more fun than perhaps you are. She looked round at me in the back of the van. 'I bet you're excited, Reuben. I didn't go to a festival till I was nineteen! And you're just seven!'

'Yes, thank you,' I said and I made a white smile.

'What an experience for these kids. Totally amazing thing for them, at such a young age,' said Auntie Jess.

'It's all so family-friendly now, isn't it?' said Mum. 'The *Guardian* says this is designed to be a family-friendly festival.'

'Praise be!' shouted Auntie Jess. 'Mothers no longer excluded from fun! Life not yet over!'

'Open the cider,' said Dad, 'I'll need a drink to get through a festival full of children.'

Ava-Grace was looking at me. She was wearing a midget vest that showed her belly and had jangly bangles on her arm like a Slinky. She did silent voice at me, making the word shapes with her mouth: *'You're a fucking weirdo.'*

'Got juice for the kids,' came Auntie Jess's voice from inside a crinkly cool bag.

'Just water between meals for my two,' hissed Mum.

'It's organic?'

'Still got natural sugars,' said Mum in the hissy snake voice again. 'They're hyped up enough already!'

I wasn't sure if I had remembered my blue ruler.

***

Driving to the Bestival, all the grown-ups were singing Radiohead, but when we got nearby, we ended up in a traffic jam that lasted for twenty hours. This is a lie as I don't have a watch yet.

'Should have had this sorted, really,' said Dad. 'They must have had an idea of numbers.'

'Let's get into our costumes!' said Mum, clambering into the back of the van. The Bestival website had told us everyone should wear costumes from the book *Alice in Wonderland*. Auntie Jess was Alice; Mum had fabric hearts stuck on her clothes as the Queen of Hearts, and Dad and Uncle Marcus had big Mad Hatter hats on. Lily was put into her Dormouse costume, which was actually my old romper suit. Mum gave me my own Mad Hatter hat, but I didn't put it on as it made me feel like I had wind in my ears, and we didn't know if anyone else would be wearing costumes yet.

'Ava's chosen not to wear a costume, haven't you, pumpkin?' said Auntie Jess.

'She looks super cool already!' shouted Mum.

Ava-Grace put her tongue up her nose. Her tongue was all shiny wet like the bottom of dead fish.

The traffic jam was so slow that we actually stopped. Dad had time to get out and to go and have a look at the lie of the land, which is what he does when he wants to smoke a roll-up cigarette. So yes, it is a lie about land.

Eventually we arrived in the Luxury Camping Area Parking and found our tent, which is like the ones the American Indians – who used the whole of the buffalo even the hooves – had but not called a tee-pee. It was called a yurt and we had hired it. Dad and Uncle Marcus made six trips to the van to get all our stuff, while Auntie Jess pulled on some boots she called Dee Ems.

'So long since I wore these. Glastonbury '92, I think.'

'For these kids, festivals will be just part of their growing up,' said Mum, who had wrapped Eden onto her front with a long bit of stripy material. Other mums have baby holders that look like rucksacks but Mum likes the wrapping material because Eden is secure when she hears Mum's heart. I don't like the sound of hearts. It makes me feel sickly like chlorine. Secure means locked.

'God. When I was little, weekends were spent sitting in some pub garden waiting for my mother to bring me a warm Coke and some prawn cocktail crisps,' said Auntie Jess.

'The additives we used to guzzle down!' said Mum. 'No wonder I have allergy problems. Reuben's skin is so much better now we've swapped him to goat's milk, by the way.'

'I noticed! You know, Ava-Grace doesn't even ask for crisps anymore,' said Auntie Jess.

I put the rice cakes that Ava-Grace had given me into my pocket very quietly. I didn't like them because they tasted like air. Air and burning.

***

The Bestival was at a place called Lulworth Castle, which is a castle like how you draw one with frilly bits at the top of towers like teeth. We walked around it. We did a lot of walking at the Bestival. Everywhere you wanted to go was on the other side of a field and all the fields were full of people lying down in the way. Mum said they were just chilling out but it was not hot, it was actually windy like when you stand close to Underground trains. On the edges of the fields were tents with flap-down bits instead of doors and you had to queue to get in, but when you got in, you would just be at the back of more people who were all waiting to see something nobody could see.

'I think it's cabaret!' said Mum in one tent. She was standing on tip-toe and looking through the crowd, holding Eden's head to her chest with one hand like she was making a Scout promise. I could only see the backs of some knees and Ava-Grace, who was making bad word shapes and bad word fingers at me.

Behind the castle there was a field Mum said was especially for children. There was a man dressed as a butterfly making children join in dancing games like at school and some cardboard boxes you could glue to other cardboard boxes and –

'Face painting!' shouted Mum. 'Oh, Reuben, let's get your face painted. All the other children are having it done!'

This was actually not true. Some children who were Lily's age had been painted to look like tigers, but the boys I saw who were about eight, which is what I nearly am, were mostly stamping on cardboard boxes.

'I don't want to.'

'What if Ava-Grace has it done too?'

'No way,' said Ava-Grace. 'I'm getting my hair braided. Mum, I need five pounds.'

'I need more cider,' said Dad. 'We'll meet you ladies back here in an hour.' He said ladies, which is not true, as I am not a lady. Lily had whiskers painted on her face and Auntie Jess was made to look like a sad clown with a sausage mouth that went down.

To be ten out of ten true, for most of the Bestival, we were just walking from one field to another. Some fields had big pink flags in them that were flying straight out in the wind, making a noise like shaking out duvets. Sometimes, we would have to sit down in the middle of the lying-down people so Dad could make a roll-up cigarette that he shared with the other grown-ups, because they were on a little holiday. I was not able to write in my notebook because Mum kept getting me to go over to other children and say hello, even though I didn't know their names. Sometimes Auntie Jess says 'What the?' and that is what I thought then. What the? I do not know what it means exactly but it has the right up-ness in the words.

In one field, there was a stage with a cover on it that was shaped like the Bat Cave. The people playing music on it were not Regina Spektor, but some of the lying-down people liked it anyway and would get up and dance on their own surrounded by all the other lying- down people. It felt like an un-true to see grown-ups dancing in the daytime. We missed the jousting display because Ava-Grace was being told off for doing inappropriate dur face at a dancing grown-up.

There were also caravans that had holes in the sides where people could queue up and buy sloppy food on paper plates. Mum bought us Tie Food, which is green and tastes of seaweed and fire. I actually wanted a

Gourmet Burger. Gourmet means extra good. You say it differently to how it looks; in this way, it is a lying word. But Mum says a burger is a burger and all burgers are made from innocent corporate cash cows that should be able to live life freely.

Mum took the empty paper plates from me and Lily to go and put them in a bin because everyone at a festival should help look after the fields. I liked looking at her when she was walking through the people, with Eden wrapped to her like a bandage. She was smaller than some mums but her apples top was the colour of the pink flags, so bright it was like shouting, and her long skirt was a whirlpool, and when I saw her I knew a secret true that she was my Mum and not other people's Mum.

Lily tried to grab the camera I was looking after. 'I want!' she said.

'I'm the oldest,' I said. This was almost an un-true as Ava was the oldest but she was being taken to the loo. I had already been taken to the loo and I didn't want to go again. When you got in, it felt tippy. The light was funny like a dirty fish tank and there was a baby smell, but Dad wouldn't come in with me and the tap on the sink was not a tap but like a gearstick. Outside, you squirted pink liquid on your hands from a machine to kill the invisible germs. You honestly couldn't see them.

I was so busy protecting the camera that when I looked up, I couldn't see my Mum any more. I stood up to be taller. It is important when doing surveillance to find good vantage points. But I still couldn't see the pink top which shouted Mum and I felt a wobble inside me like being in the tippy loo. Auntie Jess and Uncle Marcus and Dad had gone to find the tent made of beer and Mum was gone. I squeezed my right hand with my left hand because Mum will hold my right hand usually and now she was not holding it, there was an hurting empty in my hand. I suddenly knew that I must quickly run at my top speed. I grabbed Lily and pulled her along like a sledge and I was shouting 'MUM, MUM, MUM.' I had a bad un-true showing on my head screen then, saying that perhaps Mum was in an explosion like on the trains and had been made into little bits by flames. It was an un-true but I didn't know it for a fact, I had no evidence, so I had to check it by thinking about it. And this started to hurt me like the head screen was getting too big and would break its pointy edges through my skull and then a man said: 'Hey, little guy – you lost your mum?'

It was a true fact that he was a danger stranger because I didn't know him. But he had on a white suit with trousers that went big at the bottom and sunglasses made of glitter and his hair was a fuzzy multicoloured ball. It was a wig, but not a disguise, because you knew it was a wig.

'That's a wig,' I said.

'It's a disco wig,' said the man and he did a wiggle dance. 'I like to disco. What does your mum look like?'

'She is small with a top with a baby on it,' I said.

'If I hold you up high, do you think you will be able to see her?'

In times of ultimate danger, a spy has to make decisions quickly. If the Disco Man decided to run away with me, I would pull off his wig to reveal his identity and shout for the police force. I agreed to the lifting and he hoisted me up so fast I was a rocket and I zoomed up there to an amazing height. I could see heads in every direction, bobbing like bubbles in a bath, and in the distance I could even see the sea which was a little sliver of silver like a knife. Disco Man turned slowly around so he was a lighthouse and I beamed out my eyes everywhere across the Bestival and then I saw her and she was waving and running and she was a pink flag flying towards me like a race and everyone was looking around and cheering like she was winning and I was shouting: 'That's my mum! That one!'

Disco Man lowered me down like a crane and said: 'Glad to be of assistance, little buddy.'

Buddy is American for friend. Lily gave him one of the rice cakes I had given her.

***

All that day the grown-ups had been talking about the Flaming Lips. They were the headlines, they said. Headlines equals most important news. The Flaming Lips are a band that comes from America, which is where Disneyland is. I don't know if they flew on a plane from America to get to the Bestival, but we were waiting for them for so long it became dark. The field in front of the stage was filled up with millions of waiting people, who were all standing up now, and Lily was asleep in her buggy with Mum and Dad on either side of her to make sure she didn't get knocked over. I was so tired my legs were hurting like running but they kept saying the Flaming Lips would be there soon.

Something that was amazing was when the man Wayne, who is the singer in the Flaming Lips, first appeared. He was in a massive plastic bubble you could see through, like the ball that Ava's hamster goes in, and he was rolling down the steps from the Lulworth Castle, and rolling all through the standing up people, and then he went rolling right past us and

I saw that he had a white spy suit on, which I couldn't believe with my eyes but it was true. I didn't see how they opened the bubble so I can't tell you how that happens, but then he was on the stage very mini and the noise began. It wasn't like a singing noise. It was like all of the noises at once and so loud it went straight up and it filled the sky and it made the moon go small like a tiny scared eye. And there were red lasers flying out from the stage like straight lines drawn with rulers and they were out in the sky stabbing stabbing as the noises went bang bang bang bang like everything was breaking.

'Mum,' I said but she couldn't hear me. She was doing singing noises but she wasn't really singing to anyone as Uncle Marcus and Dad were finding cider and Auntie Jess was dancing.

'Mum. I want to go to the yurt now right now.'

When Mum, Lily, me and Eden left, Auntie Jess was dancing with a stranger man and Ava-Grace was sitting on the dark grass surrounded by legs like trees in a forest. She had a new henna tattoo on her tummy and she was wearing plastic ear muffs to protect her ears. She looked like a robot, sitting cross-legged and waiting for instructions, while her mum danced about in a swaying way with her sad clown face all smudged like she was melting.

'Girls night out, Ava! Just you and me, babe!' said Auntie Jess, and she leaned down to kiss Ava and some of her drink spilled.

I waved goodbye to Ava and she made the word shapes: 'Cock penis face bum' at me, but she didn't look like she meant it in a nasty way. She looked like she was wishing she was a cock penis face bum too.

***

The hired yurt was a big pointy tent that all were sleeping in together. It was a round shape inside so if you slept on the edge you had to curl yourself and if you looked at the top you could see a hole of stars. Eden was put into her basket and Lily and I had sleeping bags. Lily went to sleep straightaway because she is four, but I had my spy torch and was able to make a den inside my sleeping bag undetected, which means detectives can't find you, so I could update my grid. I added Wayne from America to my list of known white spies and, after some thought, Disco Man too. I gave Disco Man seven out of ten.

There was a little bonfire outside the yurt. When I made a hole in the top of my sleeping bag and put my eye there, I could see Mum was sitting outside on her own looking at the fire with her face all orange and black like Halloween.

I drew a picture in my notepad of Wayne's bubble and added an escape hatch just in case. When I looked again, Uncle Marcus was sitting with Mum and they were sharing a roll-up cigarette and making the grown-up murmur noises which are so hard to hear it's like a code. If I turned my head so my ear was positioned at my spy hole, some sounds would float in and I heard Mum say: 'Do you think Jess took something?' I wondered about my missing blue ruler. I still didn't know where it was but perhaps now I had a suspect. I noted this.

Then I designed a bubble that Wayne could fly back to America in and I made it have a switch that would make it invisible so you could go past explosions. Then I checked the spy hole again and Mum and Uncle Marcus had lain down backwards like they were sleeping and Uncle Marcus's head was in the way of Mum's head and his eyes were closed and he was rubbing his hand up and down Mum in a very slow way like she was poorly or a cat. Mum made a humming noise like she was dreaming and there was a weird silent feeling, a slow silent feeling, with just the crackly fire and Uncle Marcus's leg moving onto Mum's so he was lying over her, but he was moving so slowly it was like he was pretending he wasn't moving, and from somewhere else there was faraway drum music that you could feel coming through the ground. I saw her face then: it was tipped backwards; her mouth was open and her eyes were dark dark holes with just the moving lights of the flames on her so I saw her and then I didn't and she went away into the shadow and I couldn't see the pink top because it was another colour in the night-time light, not pink anymore but an un-true orange and because her bosom was and I shut both eyes because it is not good to look at un-true colours.

Sometimes when you are with your Mum and Dad, they make you do un-true things like go on the stage with the magician because they say it is fun even though the dove spikes your hands with its wire feet and tips its head to look at you with its twisty black eye and it is not fun at all. The Mum and Dad faces send a signal saying that it is fun so you make-believe it is fun but it gives you a sad inside, like when you see that Granny is wearing Grandpa's shoes again but you mustn't tell her because she has The Mentia. It is the sadness of un-trues. It is what un-trues feel like when you have to pretend they are true. They do not fit into any grid and they hang upside down in your pencil like bats and you can't put them anywhere. When I was hearing the noises of Uncle Marcus talking code to my Mum, I had a sad inside like that. It was a big sad that swelled up until the sleeping bag was a bubble that I was in, all full of sad, and I closed my eyes and I put the torch on my face so I could have the red that feels hot through my eyelids.

I may have been making the loud counting I used to make when I was a little boy as Mum came rushing up and her head was suddenly in the sleeping bag up close to mine and her breath smelled like parties.

She was snuffling like Granny's Pekinese dog. 'Darling, darling, don't do that. Mummy's here, sweetie. We're just being friendly, darling. Silly mummy being friendly, darling. One day you'll be friendly and you'll understand.'

That is not a true fact because doing something does not mean you'll understand. Understand means you can see how it works like taking the back off a clock, which my Grandpa can do. Mum said I would understand why she liked ice-skating if I did it and I did it, but I did not understand. The ice-skating boots were trying to break the bottom of my leg in the middle.

Mum rummaged around in my new silky sleeping bag until she found my wriggly hand which I had been trying to hide and she squeezed it and said: 'Reuben. Reuben. Reuben.' I knew she was saying my name times three because she couldn't find true words. I have this in my grid. And her grippy hand squeeze was like me when I had been found by the Disco Man and I thought she had died in an explosion and all I could feel was the hand space her hand wasn't in. I felt like Mum had an empty hand space and she needed me to say it was okay and that she was found now. So, even though I had the heavy sad, I took out my other hand and I put it on her hair like she does to Lily and I said: 'I'm here now, little monkey. Shush.'

In two months, I will be eight.

I don't remember after that but in my dream I was a buffalo and little children could ride on me and I looked after them until Wayne came in the bubble to give me a present to say he was my buddy.

***

The next day I was allowed a Gourmet Burger and Ava-Grace got in trouble for showing her knickers at the singer Suzanne Vega. My Mum held my right hand all day, even when we were queuing for the loo and she came in with me.

When we drove home, I fell asleep in the campervan even though Regina Spektor music was playing because Mum put it on for me.

Sometimes I would come up through the dreams and I would look out above my sleep and see everyone quiet around me in the van. Mum and Dad in the front passenger seat, and Uncle Marcus driving, and Auntie Jess in the back with an eye-mask on that has no eyeholes in it. All the grown-ups were being library silent. Eden and Lily were sleeping and Ava-Grace was using her finger on the window to trace the lines of the UK as it went past, up and down like a rollercoaster made of hills and buildings, and it was daytime and then it was evening and then it was dark time and we went under streetlights which turned us yellow then black and yellow then black and then I knew by the slowing down noises and bump under the wheels that we were up the drive and outside our own house, which is in the capital of London.

I wasn't asleep then but I wasn't awake. My body was very still and I could listen to my own breathing as if it was evidence coming from someone else. I heard Mum say: 'They're fast asleep,' and I knew Dad was coming to carry me because I could feel it tingling on my skin like Christmas Eve, and I didn't want to spoil it because it was so quiet and they were whispering but I could hear them like a perfect spy and the whispers were to look after me and keep me sleeping so I shut my eyes tight, and when he lifted me and I was in the dark of my closed eyes pretending, it was like I was really asleep and I didn't have to mind being carried, and he was my Dad again and he would take me up to bed and he was just for me and then Mum would come and tuck me in and stroke my hair and say I was her boy, her best beloved darling boy, and it was the best thing, so best that I would squeeze it down in me and hold it there forever ever like sweets. And no, I wasn't asleep but it would be like a dream when I remembered it and so it was true even if I was pretending. It was all true. It was a true thing and the best thing.

I would give that weekend a six.

43

Hollie's Dream of Consciousness

The first thing you got to know about me is that I know im not going nowhere, so you don't have to bother telling me im a waste of space because I already know. At school theres this teacher who think's as long as we got are education were all gonna be fine. well I already know where im going and that's nowere like I already told you. My name is Hollie and if I wants to put a lovehart over my i's I will, ok miss sarky lesbo.

I got 2 brothers and a sister my dad lives with this woman called sherri and I goes down my dads on weekends. My mum don't like it but tough he left and she got to live with it like we all got to. I never wanted him to go but to be fair to my dad my mums a right cow. my brother kile is a right bastard like my dad and Brandon's not much better. my sister Chantelle-Marie is a baby, so I don't bother with her much.

The 2nd thing you got to know about me is that this is my story and Ill tell it like I want to tell it and if I makes a ,mistake then tough because youre suppose to be the educated one reading it im just writting it and you cant expect to much because im a bit thick. at least im having a go. I got my rules, you got you'res but lets face it you probaly got olevels like my antie. the 3rd thing you got to know is I swear, anyone who thinks that teenages or young adults as miss sarky says anyone who thinks that teenagers dont swear is mental. I got a referral for swering in mr batesis class last week. I bet you don't know waht a referral is. its when you got to spend a day in the box or room IOI. the box is just this room

were they puts all the kids what been fighting or
swearing or settin off the fire exstinguishers and
the fire alarms and that. it really pisses them off
that do the fire exstinguishers thing because they
have to call the firemen out to fill them up again
and they put that crappy plastic tie on. I was put in
the box for telling mr Bate's to shove his homework up
his arse and I dident go to detention when he said so
he refered me. it was miss Tuckers turn in the box shes
my head of year and she give me this look like shes
all disappointed and stuff but I new it was an act.
the forth thing you got to know is that my antie
give me this typwritter because im not aloud to use
are computer anymore since the insident.she found it
in her attic and its still works and the other realy
good thing is that when I use it it anoys the crap
out of kile because it thuds threw the seelin and he
sleeps in the front room when hes on nights wich is
the room under my room and hes on nights at the
moment so I keep waking him up. If I makes a mistake
I cant go back and olter it on this thing so youll
just have to put up with it. I aint got no time to
rite it all out all over again and anyway miss
sarkys always sayin that sometimes the first drafts
are the best because that's the raw elements of the
writting or something. I like it becos it make's a
good noise.
miss sarkys so up her own arse. you can tell she just
thinks shes chocolat. She's realy into poems. i hate
poems but miss sarkys big on it. she reckons if we all
understand poems we can understand life better. I
dont think poems are gonna do me no good on the
cheese at ASDAS. by the way my mum works in ASDAS
so I can easy get a job their when I leave school.
My friends are called zoe, Alisha, Ch'niece, Kara and
Aimeigh. Ch'niece's real name is Claire but she
think's Ch'niece is more cooler so we all got to call
her Ch'niece. She got the idea off mtv. she say's
teacher's are always going on about air comma's so

she put one in stead of the a in Channiece. Shes dead
clever, Claire but the way shes carrying on with
Ryan in year I3 I wouldent bet on her getting no
gcse's. I reckon Ch'niece or Kara might get pregnant
out of us lot Ist. it wont be me you can bet your life
on that. I don't want no babies never. whats the
point? all they do is shit and piss and sick up every
where. Me and the girls are gonna be friends forever
unless one of us as a baby. which wont be me like I
said. Me and the girls been together since year 6
exsept for zoe and Ch'niece. they come from st hildas
which is the cathlic school down the road.there all
religeous in st hildas. When we come up this school
on a visit we was put in are classes and me and Kara
and Aimeigh was put in the same class as zoe and
Claire. See, kile told me that if you put down your
best friends names they splits you up when you comes
to comp he reckons its divine and rule or something
I don't know I dident understand.kile knows about
stuff like that all posh words.he listens to radio 4
so god knows why he drives a taxi he shoud be in
university I reckon but he dosent think universities
a valuble way to spend his time. id love to go to
university but I don't think its on the cards realy.
I've mucked about to much. anyway its only a doss for
three years before you gets a job anyway so I might
as well earn money strataway. my antie said she had
the best time ever at university, but even thow I no
I probaly get into the drinking side of it im not so
keen on writting essays. that's how I come to be
writing this, I was downstairs in the living room
and I had this essay to write about shakepeer and my
antie was over and she said she'd give me an and so
I told her what I ad to do and she went on about
something I dident understand and I just went "why
cant he just write it proper so I can understand and
she said maby I shud write something myself and so
that's what im doing. anyway so me and Kara and
Aimeigh kept quiet and we eneded up in the same

class. miss green wasent happy. She did this thing
with her mouth and you could see all the lines
around her lips where her foundation lumps up in
the creases. so I reckon me and the girls will be
friends for life. mind you if one of them haves a
baby im not sure I'll visit. I do'nt like babies much.
my sisters a baby and all she does is make noise.
Brandon and Kile thinks shes the best thing ever
but I dont. my mum dont even talk to me no more
unless shes yelling at me. I gets enough of being
yelled at in school. ok its usuly my fault, but at
home I got to be quiet because of chantelle marie and
Kile aswell like I said but mum dont go mad if I
wakes up kile. I cant have no fun at home no more
since chantelle-marie was born. The girls aint aloud
to come over no more and if I goes out I got to be back
before Chantelle-Marie goes down for the night so I
dont wake her up when I gets back. I tell you that
kid is ruining my life. brandon and Kiles ok. they
got there job's and there aloud to come and go
whenever they like. mum dont mind because they
brings home money every week like. mum only got a
part time job on the cheese at ASDAS and when I gets
my job down there I'll pay my share but till then I
got to live by mums rules like she keeps telling me.
what shall I start with? what do you want to now?
you now what schools like and I told you about my
family see this is the problem. its all very well my
antie telling me to write my own story but im not
that good at it as you probaly noticed by now. miss
sarkys always on at me to spell right and use
puctuation and gramma and that but honest I dont
get it. its all rules and thing's but the way I see it
if you can get what someones saying whats the
problem? Miss sarkys not her real name of corse you
new that dident you? her names Ms trent. I could
always tell you about the time me and Kara mitched
of school and went down the rec and this wino told
us of for sitting on his bench. Or theres this time

47

when Ch'niece got so pissed on magners she puked on zoes bare feet in the park. that was last summer.Then theres the time Brandon cort me and the girls doing speed over the sheds. but I dont think you would like those storys anyway I already told you really.
Yesterday was good. Me and Ch'niece mitched of assemberly, there was a bloke giving out bibles. by the way, im stopping in a minute. mum come up ten minutes ago and said i had to pack it in for the night so i have to or she wont let me go up Aimeigh's tomorrow. this is a bit like a dairy i suppose. My antie reads famous peoples dairies. Maby i can be like that Victoria Wolf she told me about, the one what does the dream of consiousness. I liked that. anyway im off now. goodnite.

* * *

Miss sarky told me i had potential today. Shes been on at me for 3 years telling me i got to do this and I got to do that Then today she askes me to stay behind and Kara's going yeah, good luck HOLLIE So i wasent going to get my break because Miss Sarky wanted to see me so i wasn't in the best mood and then she comes over all serious and goes "Now Hollie, what are you going to take for your options next year and im going i don't know. my mum's allways saying that gcse's dont mean nothing but i got to do em. My dad still reckons that if i got GCSE's I got a chance but what would he no working on the bins anyway, I dont think he ever had to do no power point presentation in the interview for that job. But im not gonna go collage and im not staying on for 6 form. But I should have asperations aparently. Miss sarky said I dont have to work on the cheese and i got to admit the way miss sarky was going on i could do anything I wanted. Then she showed me my essay what I done last week on Romeo and Juliet for my year 9 corsework folder. She asked us to write weather we thort Romeo

was really in love with Juliet or weather we just
thinks he wants to get into her knickers. Well, that
wasent the heading but that's the gist of it like.
She told me my ideas were spot on but my spelling was
crap and my punctuation was crap aswel. She never
said crap she said if i tried to sort out the basics
i could achieve more. i told her my antie helped
loads and ms Trent goes if i'd of payed attention to
the detail i'd of got a level 6. she said if i get a
level 6 in the end of year asesments i'll go into the
middle group next year not the duppers. She says
she'll help me any time I like to catch up on the
stuff I need to know. Anyway at the end of miss
sarky's little talk i never said nothing. i dont
reckon I can get level 6. Rachel Jenkins gets level
6 all the time, but she reads books for fun.
Oh i know what i was gonna tell you. Kile come home
yesterday and hes got this girl up the duff. He
hav'ent been seeing her or nothing he jst shagged
her this once and she's up the duff. How funny is
that. NOT. Kile wants her to move in with us and mum
said yes. That's so sad. So Kile and this Tammi-Leigh's
gonna move into the downstairs front full time and
Brandon gets the big bedroom all to himself. Nice.

* * *

Me and Kara mitched off school today. i had another
lesson booked with miss sarky at dinnertime but
whatever. We went to Reg and got our marks and then
we went down the town outside Morrison's. Kara had
some vodka and I nicked some coke out of the fridge
so we sat on the grass by the trollies and got pissed.
It was wicked. I sicked up at about eleven but then I
had a pasty which helped. Kara was face down in the
grass and I thought she was going to suffercate but
then she burped up some sick and she was allright
after. Some st Hildas come round but when they saw us
by the trollies they went. I got a text off Ch'Niece

saying that Mr Frazer come into catering to give me a letter so he knows I'm mitching. That means another day in the box. Miss Trent will be gutted. She's been really nice to me since she started teaching me dinnertimes. I felt a bit gilty. I sicked up again before I come home tonight but no-one give a toss where i been. Chantelle-Marie been breathing funny so there all doing there nut about her.

* * *

I've been selected for a project. Ms Trent said that it would be benifitial for me to work outside the classroom enviroment so she put my name forward for the World book day thing. I'm not sure. There's gonna be kids from St Leonards, and St Michaels so I wouldn't know anyone. The only other Year 9 going from our school is Dewi Clarke. He's a geek. then again he might give me some weed if we're there together. i can swap that for some vodka. Tammi's getting really massive now. It's the ugliest thing I ever seen. Her belly's all huge like someone shoved a fitball up her top and she gets all red when anyone mentions it. She's quite pretty really but then once you gets past her face there's this ginormous big round belly sticking out and it's disgusting. She's massive. She keeps rubbing herself as well. I feel sick just looking at her. She asked me the other day if I wanted to feel the baby kicking and I just looked at her. She's only a year older than me and she was talking to me like she knows loads more than me and I was thinking yeah but who's thick enough to get fucked and pregnant? Maby I will go on that project. Sorry for being away so long but it's all been going off. Ms Trent got all annoyed with me because I told her I got to get a job straight after GCSEs. She had some idea that I could go to College and I was thinking that might be ok, but then it all went off. Kile and Tammi have split up and Mum got the sack off ASDA for nicking booze stupid cow. Luckily they never phoned the police but she got the sack and she's not even allowed to do her big shop down there anymore. She got to go down Morrison's which annoys me because that's my place for getting pissed with the girls. Means my job on the cheese is out as well. I'll have to get a job somewhere else so I can give money to mum because all Kile's money's going to go on Child Support soon as that baby's born. Poor bastard. It never had a chance to start with and then him and Tammi-Leigh go and split up anyway. Brandon got arrested for breaking into a car and trying to steal a lap top. Turned out it was just a lap top bag with no lap top in it, the tool. He got 3 months so there's no money coming in from him. When I tried to explain all this to Miss sarky, she just went "Oh well, you never stick at anything, do you Hollie" like it was my fault. I won't be able to finish my story now because I'm going to be so busy, so maybe Ms Trent's right. I can't stick at anything. I'm proud of what I've wrote though. Kara, Aimeigh and that lot haven't got no story, have they? And I've learnt loads off Ms Trent so I don't need to go to College. I got to stick around because my family's going right down the pan and it's only me what's going to sort it. Me. Hollie. You better watch out for me. It's only me what's got any sense.

CHERYL ALU

The Betsy

We didn't know for sure that Dad was having an affair until he took us to lunch with her. The Mistress. 'How soap-opera can you get?' says my sister Janelle. The other thing she says at least forty times a day is, 'I told you so.' I hate her when she does that, but it's hard to hate her because she looks just like me. We're identical twins. Except she's the pretty one.

Betsy acted surprised when she saw us at the mall with Dad.'What a coincidence running into you here, Richard,' she said.

It was weird hearing a total stranger say my father's name like that. The way she said it – as if it were written in italics. I felt Janelle's breath at my ear whispering *Bingo!*

'Well … hey, you. How are you?' Dad was using his phony-natural voice. Like when he talks to a teacher at parent-teachers night and nods a lot and says *yes, they are good girls*. Or when he's at work in the showroom trying to close the deal on some ugly green station wagon and he says, *You're going to love this car. If you don't, I'll buy it back from you.*

'Girls, this is Betsy. A friend of mine. Betsy, my daughters Janelle and Kylie.'

She was wearing a dark-blue suit like it was her first day at a new job in a bank. Or a funeral home. I figured she thought the outfit made her look old enough to be with my father. 'Be with?' Janelle said to me later, laughing. 'Don't you mean fucking his brains out?'

'So, you two must be twins,' says the Betsy person. Janelle and I get that all the time. It's so dumb and I think she was sorry she said it because she immediately followed it up with, 'I mean, you're both so beautiful. Both of you.'

Then Janelle said, 'Wow, Dad. What are the chances of seeing a friend of yours at the mall? Especially when you hate the mall and never want to go and yet today you insisted on coming along. Kind of spooky, isn't it?'

Janelle was being a bitch. I love it when she does that because she's really good at it, and as long as I'm not on the receiving end, she can be damn funny. Then Dad said, 'But isn't that the very definition of coincidence, Janelle?' He gave me a wink and laughed a little and so did The Betsy and so did I. A little. Then we all just stood there listening to mall music.

During the hundred years it took us to order and eat a pizza I hardly spoke. I wanted to be anywhere but where I was. I wanted to be with J.D. I thought about him all the time now. It was too much. I kept seeing him sitting on the floor of his room playing the same chords over and over on his guitar. Or moving around in there with the little bed and desk that he'd outgrown. He'd told me he owned eight guitars and had a birthmark in the shape of a guitar on his thigh. When I saw it I didn't think it looked at all like a guitar, but I said, Oh yeah, cool anyway.

There was a cute Mexican boy mopping the restaurant floor and smiling at me as he spread the smell of ammonia everywhere. It hung in the recycled air and mixed with the garlic. I smiled back at him. Dad and Betsy seemed unable to stop talking. They agreed that it most likely would rain on the weekend and that they didn't think gas prices would ever come down. Neither one of them had seen the new Clint Eastwood movie but they were sure they would. They laughed about a typo on the menu — *coal* slaw put them over the edge. They agreed the Atkins diet wasn't all that healthful and that wicker furniture was a bad investment. It just kept going like that – yakking about a lot of nothing. Then when Betsy started to tell a story about her cat that's when Janelle let out an audible groan. She rolled her eyes and Dad said her name without looking at her and kept right on smiling at Betsy-face.

I wanted to say something. I wanted to be charming and phony-natural like Dad, but everything I thought of to say sounded too nice and would've made this Betsy person like me, and that would've pissed off Janelle. Or else whatever I thought of to say sounded too mean and would've made Dad angry. *Is it so hard to try and make people like you?* I didn't need to hear that again.

I could tell he regretted arranging this coincidence of his. The way his knee was bouncing more than usual and how he seemed to not like the taste of barbequed chicken pizza anymore. He must've seen an upside to introducing his children to his mistress, but what that was, exactly, is hard to say. Whatever he thought would happen didn't seem to be happening. Poor Dad. But I guess it's really Mom I should be feeling sorry for.

The Mexican kid still was mopping, lingering too long near our table. I realized it had been Janelle he was smiling at because he stared at her now and she was very careful to avoid making eye contact. I stared at the date on my watch, for lack of anything else to look at, and counted. It had been exactly five days and seventeen hours since the party at Kristal's house. Her dad and stepmother were gone, as usual, and the living room was filled with people and music and smoky light. Out back in the Jacuzzi there was her brother J.D., and two other guys he said were in his band. J.D.'s thirty and back living with his father in the house where he grew up. His wife had just kicked him out and he said he thinks this time she means it.

'Hey, saved you a seat,' he had said, as I was taking off my jeans and tee-shirt and climbing into the Jacuzzi. The water was hotter than I thought I could stand, but soon it didn't feel so hot and then it felt good. Everything felt good sitting close to J.D. I'd had a crush on him since Kristal and I were in the sixth grade, but I didn't think he knew I was alive. We sipped from the same beer bottle and I felt his leg touch mine under the water. I liked the deliberate feel of it. He slid down low beside me and leaned his head on my shoulder and closed his eyes.

'Which one are you?' he said, almost as if he were talking in his sleep.

'Guess.' I said.

He moved his arm around my waist and pulled me closer.

'Hmm … let's see … you feel like the Kylie one.'

I was very glad he got it right.

Janelle insisted on having dessert just to prolong the torture. The Betsy (Janelle named her that and if you knew her, you'd appreciate how perfect a name it is, and how Janelle can be a genius sometimes about things like nailing a person with a nickname) didn't have a clue. She and Dad had run out of meaningless things to talk about and she seemed to be expecting him to do something. To make something happen. She took ridiculously tiny bites of food and made sure she swallowed before laughing at almost everything Dad said. Then Dad would look at us as if to say, See? Your old man is pretty damn funny after all.

Looking at Janelle across the table you would've sworn it was her birthday and that there was a table full of gifts in front of her instead of three very uncomfortable people. But nothing gets her going like other people's misery. Dad was having an affair just like she'd been saying and now he'd done this incredibly stupid thing that proved her right. Janelle was happy. I could tell it amused her the way The Betsey was trying hard to keep from touching my father. She stabbed her straw into the ice cubes in her glass and giggled. She kept forcing her gaze away from him and back to us because it was us she was speaking to, but not who she wanted to be looking at.

Finally, I thought of something to say. 'Do you have any kids?'

Betsy kept chewing on that olive longer than I thought possible. She seemed to not know the answer. Then it came to her. The answer was, no, she didn't have any kids. And, I guess, that was all she could think of to say about it.

'Oh, that's too bad,' Janelle said, with a little wiggle, inching forward in her seat. She looked at me, eyes shining as if to say, 'Good one, Kylie!'

'Because if you had kids then we could meet them and we could all be friends. I mean, how great would that be? Are you sure you don't have kids?' Janelle knew that would crack me up.

I had to press hard to keep my lips together and the Pepsi from spraying out. Dad was about to say something, but instead he pulled out his wallet and walked over to the cashier to pay the bill even though he knew the waitress would take his money. The Betsy watched him for a second then gave us a grin and dabbed at her perfectly crumbless lips with a paper napkin that said, *Bobo's — We Deliver.*

'So, how do you know my dad? I mean how did you meet him? Did you buy a car from him? A Cadillac?' Janelle tossed out each question like a dart.

The Betsy just blinked a bunch of times and said that no, she did not buy a car from him. But she did test drive one. 'A white one. With red leather interior,' she added, helpfully. 'I'm still thinking about it though. Cadillac certainly makes lovely automobiles.'

Dad came back to the table with a toothpick in his mouth and mints for everybody. He stood behind his chair, holding it tight with both hands. 'Great seeing you, Betsy. Real nice ... really. Sorry we have to run.'

She stood up abruptly. She looked somehow relieved and disappointed all at the same time.

Janelle said, 'I hope you decide to buy that car. I'm sure you'll love it and if you don't, Dad will buy it back from you. Right, Dad?'

Dad looked at Janelle the way he sometimes does, as if he has no idea who she is. Without thinking, I stuck out my hand and said, 'Nice meeting you, Betsy.' She took my hand and looked at me as if I'd just dedicated a song to her.

'Well, it was certainly lovely meeting you all too.' Then she looked at my father and just said, 'Richard.'

I wasn't a bit surprised that mom brought home barbequed chicken pizza for dinner that night. She has a way of doing weird things without even knowing how weird they are. I set the table while she tap-tapped around the kitchen in her high-heels making a salad. She hadn't changed out of her work clothes yet. She was wearing one of those sexy-but-business-like suits all the real estate women wear. Lately, whenever we're alone she pumps me for information about Janelle. My sister seems to be a puzzle my mother can never solve.

'It's a simple question, Kylie, does she or does she not have a boyfriend?'

'How would I know?'

'Don't be coy. Of course you'd know. She tells you everything.'

I doubted that, but I wished it were true. My mother slid the hot pizza out of the box. It didn't look good. It was misshapen and too red and all the cheese seemed to be only on one side of it. My mother looked at me with sad eyes and said, 'It slid off the car seat on the way home.'

'Don't worry. I'm sure it still tastes great,' I said.

At the dinner table, nobody said a word about having had pizza for lunch. Mom talked for a while about the condo she sold that afternoon and Dad made a few pointless remarks about interest rates then nobody said much of anything for a long time. Janelle broke the silence saying how good the pizza was. Everyone agreed. Then she said, 'I think I like this pizza so much I could eat it twice in one day.' I kept my eyes on my grease-stained napkin. She took another bite and asked Dad if he liked barbequed chicken pizza enough to eat it twice in one day too.

He looked at her for several long minutes and when he finally spoke he sounded kind of tired. 'I never really thought about it, Janelle, but I guess if you held a gun to my head, yes, I suppose I could eat it twice in one day.'

Then we were all quiet again. Everybody just chewing.

'So. How was the mall? Buy anything?' said Mom.

Janelle stood up and carried her plate to the sink. 'No. Dad wouldn't let me have the Nikes I wanted. But maybe he'll change his mind.'

She came back behind Dad's chair and leaned down, sliding her arm across his chest, and gave him a peck on the cheek. 'Will you, Dad? Will you change your mind?'

Janelle and I smoked the last of her pot and I told her I wanted to go to Kristal's and listen to J.D.'s band practice. He had asked me the day before. It would be the first time I'd seem him since the night of the party.

Janelle laughed. 'He has a band? What about his wife and kid?'

'I don't think they're in the band,' I said.

'Real funny. What about his job? Doesn't he work any more?'

'His lawyer made him quit.'

Janelle nodded thoughtfully. 'Nice,' she said, meaning what a jerk. 'Okay. Here's what you do. Go and act totally natural. Otherwise, if you don't go he'll think you're angry or freaked or something. You can't change what happened but you can change the way you look at it.' That was one of Janelle's philosophies that you can pretty much plug into any situation and sound like you're saying something profound. Sometimes it makes me feel better and sometimes it doesn't.

I could hear the music before I turned the corner. The band was set up inside the garage and playing a J.D. original. The same song he had played for me that night in his room. It only took me seconds to spot Deena. Dizzy Deena J.D. called her. He'd said like all beautiful women, she was insane and that she was the reason his wife had put all his stuff out on the front lawn and changed the locks. He said he wished he'd never met her and was trying to break up with her, but he had to do it slowly or she'd kill herself.

I don't know how I knew that that was her but I did. She was the only person sitting in a chair. It was one of those low to the ground beach chairs and her long legs seemed to have nowhere to go. She was drinking from an oversized plastic martini glass and not trying to hide how bored she was. She played with her hair, twisting it into a fat black shiny knot and then slowly shaking it loose. She didn't seem interested enough in J.D. or anything else to even bother killing herself. There were lots of other people there, some of them I knew and some I didn't. I went into the house to find Kristal but she wasn't home. No one was there, but with dirty dishes on the table and newspapers piled up in the corner and the dryer going it seemed as if the house had been abandoned in a hurry. I went back outside and stood around in the driveway and moved through the small crowd listening to the music in front of the open garage.

I didn't sit down on the grass until I was sure J.D. had seen me. When his girlfriend wasn't looking, he gave me a nod. I knew it was a signal, I just didn't know what it meant. J.D. kept his eyes closed while he played. I wondered how he could stand it – being back living in this house. Being in this very garage where his mother committed suicide. I remembered that he was the one who had found her in her car, dead from the exhaust fumes. I went to her funeral and I think that's when I fell in love with him. The sadness on his face made him so beautiful to me. I remember standing next to Kristal in church and praying to God to send her mother to heaven and to forgive me for having indecent thoughts about her brother.

The old Harley that belongs to J.D.'s dad had been moved out of the garage to make room for the band. It was parked in the driveway near where I sat on the grass. I could see the whole scene – J.D., the band, the people watching them, the yellow streetlights – all of it reflected small and bent in the bright chrome fender.

When almost everyone had gone, J.D. and Deena had a private conversation by the side of the house. Something he said made her laugh, but even laughing she looked angry. She got into her car and drove away, blowing right through the stop sign at the corner. He wouldn't tell me what they talked about, later, when we were lying on the bed in his room listening to some band I'd never heard of. 'We can have sex or we can talk about Deena. We can't do both,' he said.

We were surrounded by J.D.'s stuff from when he was a kid, sports trophies and rock posters with the colours all faded away. And there were other things in there too. Things that must've belonged to his mother. A sewing machine and cookbooks and ladies'- shoe boxes. And there were Christmas lights and a carton of his dad's motorcycle magazines stacked in the corner and some cigars that J.D. said his dad's new wife wouldn't let him smoke in the house. J.D.'s room looked like a place where they put things they didn't know what else to do with.

'So what's going on with your sister?' he said, pulling himself out of his tee shirt. 'She home tonight?'

Yesterday Janelle went to Hawaii with her soccer team. I helped her pack. She took those Nikes Dad finally let her buy along with two new Juicy bathing suits. Even though we look alike, we're not, really. Janelle loves to play sports. I hate sports. I hate to sweat. Whenever she's away on these trips with her swim team or her soccer team or her softball team, I try to send her a thought message. Communicate telepathically the way twins are supposed to be able to do. But I think I do this more to make sure she *can't* read my mind.

After that first night with J.D., Janelle seemed to already know what happened before I said a word. As soon as I came in she started with the questions. She's the only one I told what happened – how we'd had sex and how I wasn't really sure I'd wanted to do it but I didn't do anything to stop it. At first she was angry because she said she had wanted to be the first one to do it. But then her curiosity took over and she stopped being mad and made me repeat the details endlessly. And she's right. It's better not to have made a big deal out of it. He was just my first and what's the point of freaking out mom and dad? 'Nobody's first time is ever as great as they imagine it will be even if the guy is someone you've lusted after forever,' Janelle said. 'And, after all, you liked it, didn't you?'

'Take Janelle's old bathing suit. It's so much cuter than that one you have.' My mother tosses the pink and yellow print bikini at me. I'm packing for a trip to visit my grandmother in Palm Springs. 'And please, no baggy pants,' she says, walking out of my room. My mother wishes Janelle and I still dressed alike.

On the road. This trip is supposed to make up for Janelle getting to go to Hawaii. I guess this makes sense to them because Gram has a pool. And it's hot there. And there're palm trees. I'm sitting in the back of my dad's new Escalade. He gets a new car to drive every year from the dealership. His gym bag is on the floor behind his seat and I push at it with my foot. It's open and I can see a package of condoms in there beside a clean white towel and a Power Bar. Janelle had told me about the condoms. That was her first clue.

I try to picture my dad and The Betsy and what they might do when they're together. It suddenly occurs to me that maybe it was her idea that we all should meet. Maybe she wanted to know what she was dealing with.

We have a two-hour drive ahead of us so I stretch out on the seat and close my eyes. I work on getting a mental picture of the restaurant I know we'll go to tonight with Gram. It's the only place she likes to go. The owner is her friend Leo, and there are pictures of him with old movie stars on the walls. Whenever we eat there Leo always gives us free gelato for dessert, and he always asks my Gram to marry him. I try to remember some of the Italian words my Gram taught me so I can say them to Leo later, but it's too hard to concentrate with my mother and father talking.

'Why can't you just admit it?' says Dad.

Without looking at him my mother says, 'You asked me if I turned it off and I did, and I told you that I did.'

'I asked you if you unplugged it and you said you did but you didn't. You lied.'

'I did not lie.'

'Yes, you did. You didn't unplug it. I know you didn't because I went back and unplugged it myself.'

They're quiet for a while and all I can hear is the white noise of the air-conditioner. The leather seat feels cool against my cheek and smells clean like a man's cologne. My eyes are still closed, but I can tell that my mother turned around to look at me. But she's not looking at me any longer.

Then my mother says, 'You don't have to unplug an iron. You can just turn it off. I turned it off.'

'Well, turning it off and unplugging it are two different things, aren't they?'

'No, not necessarily.'

'Jesus Christ. You can't help yourself, can you? You have to lie. It's just your nature.'

'You're a jackass, okay? I'm sick of it. I'm sick of hearing the same shit from you all of the time.'

'You're a liar. You lie to your own mother.'

'I lied to my mother to see you, you prick.'

'Calm down, will you? You'll wake Kylie up.'

'She's not sleeping.'

'Her eyes are closed, aren't they? She's sleeping.'

'No she isn't,' my mother said. 'A person can have their eyes closed and not be sleeping.'

When I was a lot younger and before we moved into the big house, my dad worked the night shift at a factory. I would often fall asleep beside my mother in their bed. Then, when my father came home late at night he would pick me up and carry me back to the bed I shared with Janelle. That would always wake me, but I never opened my eyes. I always pretended to be still asleep and I would let him carry me.

This is an amazing vehicle, I've heard my father tell people. *You'd swear there was no road at all under the wheels.* And that's exactly how it does feel, but it's not a feeling I like.

This is when I should do it. I should tell him I'm not asleep. Tell him she's right. A person can have their eyes closed and not be asleep. How can you not know that? I wait for myself to say this because somebody should. Somebody should say the truth. But the moment passes. I try hard to think of Janelle and what she might be doing right now. I try to send her a thought message, but instead I get a picture of J.D. His face is hovering over me. He's about to have an orgasm and I'm surprised all over again how mean the face of love can look. I open my eyes to make J.D. go away and I sit up straight on the seat that's way too big for a normal human body. I can see my dad's eyes in the rear view mirror. He looks at me, then back to the road, concentrating on the empty stretch of gray freeway. My mother stares out the side window. It's hard to know what she sees.

ANNA BRITTEN

On Creation

Launch minus 7 days

I won't stop. In my motorcycle side mirror, Shawn's pickup bears down on me. Every few moments my cell vibrates in my pocket, but he knows I can't answer while I'm on my motorcycle so now and then he leans out the window to yell 'Stop' and 'Honey, please...' but no profanities because he's real polite and I'd be the first person to say so.

Guess he searched my bathroom trash: and found the evidence – snapped in two, parcelled in toilet tissue and stuffed into an empty Olay jar. And then worked out why it was there.

See, the pee was still warm on the stick, and the stick still sitting on the cistern, when my cell rang. It was Captain Galbraith: 'Leto? This is it.'

Four words. But those four words zoomed through and behind me at the speed of light. Back, back, back to the little me sitting on Gramma's green corduroy couch in Tallahassee with my brother's *My Big Book Of Space* open on my lap. And that little me, she lifted up her pigtailed head and said *You're frickin' kidding me!* How could I let her down?

'Del Bosque threw his back out last night shooting hoops with his son,' continued Galbraith. 'We can't ignore the evidence – he can't fly. Poor guy, we've scratched him. You're his designated backup. Don't expect a Christmas card from him this year, will you?'

After I hung up I figured I ought to check the stick. I'd had a preflight medical exam ten days ago, standard procedure, and was deemed officially without child. But there it was, the word 'pregnant' in blue. They do in words nowadays not lines, because apparently the lines confused dumb chicks.

I didn't panic. Glycoproteins and pigments, that's all this amounted to — I know how these kits work, being a chemical engineer. A degree (the first Leto ever to get one), a masters, then two year's rookie astronaut training in simulators, lecture halls and supersonic jet trainers. Then seven years waiting for the call – this call.

Pregnant women aren't allowed in space. This is because radiation and toxin exposure, decompression sickness and the effects of microgravity might put the embryo at risk. Might. Either way, I am expected to turn myself in. Trusted.

They weren't scratching me. I chose to ignore the evidence.

So I opened the bathroom door and found Shawn waiting there with the same psyched look he'd worn since my period failed to arrive two days ago.

'What's happening? Are we having a baby?'

'There is no baby. I'm going into space.'

And now, tailing me down the lane and onto the highway, he wants to reverse both those statements. He glides up alongside me, doing about 30, like we're in some senior citizen remake of *Bullitt*.

'You're risking our baby's life,' he calls, barely audible over the roar of the interstate traffic up ahead.

'It's not a baby – it's a blob. Go home!'

I lose him at Exit 212, wheeling through the gridlock like a firework.

In my bedroom at the quarantine facility a doctor asks me questions. *Have you had intercourse since your last medical examination?* Negative, sir. They trust me. No one at NASA even knows I have a boyfriend. Afterwards I listen to 'Born To Run' on my iPod. Shawn texts me: *This thing is bigger than you. Talk to me.* Later: *I love children. Why else do you think I teach eighth grade?* And at midnight: *Remember someone down here loves you.*

Launch Day

After a dinner none of us can swallow, we suit up and board a bus for the ten-minute drive to the waiting shuttle, our path cleared by a security helicopter and armed escorts.

Half a mile away, I see her — vast and glinting. She is so close I long to run and touch her. Through the window a flashlight slices through the darkness and at first I panic that it's Shawn. It isn't – but it might be someone alerted by him. A security guard climbs aboard, and walks down the aisle staring at us each in turn. He stops next to me.

'Someone on this bus is keeping quiet about something,' he barks.

Oh God. I, so close to my dream I can smell its propellant, feel my cheeks begin to smoulder.

'Somebody thought she could slip quietly in here today without any fuss.'

My voice cracks as I stammer sorry and fumble for the words to explain myself. *A-a-ambition…*

The rest of the crew stare at me, rolling their eyes. Here's Leto, the rookie reserve, about to be pulled off the bus, and throw the whole mission into jeopardy, because she couldn't keep her panties up.

They stare and stare until sweat breaks out on my forehead then Galbraith finally cracks a smile, and then Cobley does, and soon enough the whole bus is shaking with laughter.

'Susanna Leto,' says the guard. 'On behalf of all at Mission Control I'd like to congratulate you on becoming the youngest female astronaut to take part in a US space mission. Way to go. This is for you.'

A bouquet of white roses appears on my lap along with a giant card depicting my face superimposed on the side of the shuttle. I cover my face with it and scream as moths KO themselves against the window.

Lift off minus thirty seconds

We are now burning fuel. Our fates are no longer ours to decide. Thank God or whatever.

One by one our bonds are loosened with the Earth – its computers, its oxygen, its gigantic nuts and bolts all yield in turn. It is the longest farewell.

From Mission Control Center we hear the final checklist being called out, each item answered with a single word: *Go*. Just one *No Go* and we're beached, but today it's *Go* all the way. *Go* — *Go* — *Go*.

My training means nothing about lift off is a surprise and yet as the force shoves me back into my seat and my headset fills with static I am filled with bilious panic. Can I really pull this off?

The chasm between nothing and creation. How do we traverse it without losing our balance and plummeting to oblivion? And even if we survive – who knows how different we may be when we return?

Eight minutes after lift off we are in space. Thirteen days away from home.

I try to forget what's inside me by focusing on what's outside. But my heart feels like a kite snagged on a branch.

How the hell did this happen to me? Like all female astronauts, I take the heaviest dosage Pill on the market. I scan the past fortnight in my mind – there was that afternoon I threw up after Shawn's sister's birthday barbecue on account of too much mortadella and frozen yoghurt. I remember thinking it was OK, that I would have absorbed the all-important, Blob-blocking ethinylestradiol and gestodene by then. Hah.

I fumble towards a mental list of options. Top is 'Forget Blob'. Blob is still arguably nothing more than a late period. Blob is no bigger a deal than earwax.

Flight Day Two
Gynaecology – the final frontier
Every time I need to pee – which is often – I clip myself to the toilet and pull the bars over my thighs to hold me in place. Every time, I wonder if my exiting the earth's atmosphere has caused Blob to exit mine. I'd know for sure – in space you bleed just the same.

I suck some lemonade out of a vacuum pack and push some freeze-dried potato into my mouth. So hungry. 'Hey! That's man food. Girl food is under there,' says Galbraith pointing. Sludgily, I lift my hand to my throat, mortified. 'I'm joking,' he laughs.

I sleep in a sleeping bag stuck to the cabin wall. One night I'm thinking about the 1969 moon landing, and how Mrs Armstrong, Mrs Aldrin and Mrs Collins dressed in red, white and blue to greet their husbands. They pressed their fingers to the window of the quarantine area and wept as their men smiled, all of them knowing nothing would ever be the same again. Inevitably I dream about Shawn, that I'm staring down on him lying on the roof of his apartment building, where's he's gazing into the night sky and wearing the old Bruce Springsteen t-shirt. The one he was wearing the day we met six months ago at a children's science fair. The one that says *Tramps like us baby we were born to run* with no punctuation. The one that made me say, 'Who said scientists were illiterate?' and made him put his warm palm against my cheek in a gesture I found overfamiliar at the time. In the dream he can't see me. I wake up with a sore throat, like I've been hollering for hours.

I suck down more lemonade and eat some bran flakes, feeling sick with guilt or progesterone, I can't tell which.

Gotta revisit that list of options. 'Forget Blob'? – *No Go.*

Flight Day Six
At 8.44am, Galbraith detects a puncture in the heat shield. If it's not fixed, hot gases will pour in and we could burn up when we hit the earth's atmosphere. This is what did for Columbia in 03. It is probably something infinitesimally small, no bigger than a pinhole. But in space, in a vacuum without gravity, small things grow into big things and *blam* game over.

'We're putting this top of the work docket,' says Galbraith, a note of panic in his voice. After a pause: 'Some of us have got kids down there.'

A spacewalk is planned for the next morning. Nobody sleeps.

Flight Day Seven

Cobley is swaddled in his space suit and strapped onto the space station's robotic arm, which I am controlling from the aft flight deck. I have a translational controller in my left hand and a rotational controller in my right; my arms are stretched across the grey bank of switches and dials. If we burn up now I'll die hugging a machine. There's folks on Earth who'd find that real ironic.

And yet I feel close to Cobley, too. It's hard to explain – like something clawing at my chest, pulling the skin clear of my ribs. At the first glimpse of him on the monitors I gasp. He looks like a snowman at the end of a white umbilical cord. My fingertips position him onto the starboard side of the forward section and I try not to look into the blackness behind him for fear my heart will stop. I focus so hard on this vulnerable human being that I forget to breathe.

Cobley says he's found something and it looks weird.

Quelling a growing shake across my whole body, I focus anew on the instruments in front of me.

'Holy...' I say.

'Hold on, guys. Just hold on,' says Galbraith.

'OK weird,' says Cobley. 'Not end-of-the-world weird.' Over the course of an hour he tugs clear several strips of ceramic fiber cloth jutting out from between the heat-resistant tiles lining the shuttle's belly. We're safe.

And then, as I am preparing to carry him back inside, the monitor goes blank. My mind follows.

'We've lost visual,' I say, my mouth dry. I reel off all the obscenities I have ever heard. I burn to see Cobley. Where is he? If I could just see him everything would be OK.

Someone snaps the monitor switch on and off, taps it. Someone else pushes a straw into my mouth and I suck water.

I swallow hard and ask Cobley to tell me where he needs to be. *A fraction to the left; now straight ahead.* Say when. Say it's all right. I am a blind mother teaching a blind child to walk. He is inches from the hatch when the monitor flickers at last back to life. The sight of him, white as a hotel facecloth, makes me crow with joy. When Cobley is locked safely

66

back inside the shuttle's belly, our numb, exhausted silence is broken only from the applause over the radio from Mission Control.

'Hit the treadmill, Leto,' says Galbraith. 'You look like you need a break.'

Launch minus two days

We're going home. Re-entry: the syllables slide like a palette knife under my veneer.

Cobley goes to close the porthole – I stop his arm.

The earth, hanging there. As helpless as a bubble. As helpless as Blob.

Space is monochrome; but Earth is blue and white and gold and glittery. All three of us look at it through the telephoto lens of the camera a long time, unable to speak.

'If we *don't* make it back, at least we saw this,' I say, my chest aching.

With the naked eye Earth is the size of a thumbnail. I can just blot it out — like that. Rising over the moon's horizon, it is half in, half out of the black nothingness. I think of Shawn's bare, freckled shoulder rising from the duvet as he stretches for the TV remote, switching on the breakfast news to watch me.

'Look how lucky we are,' says Galbraith. 'Humans got the best damn real estate in the universe.'

'We're beautiful,' says Cobley. 'Aren't we? Beautiful. And nothing.'

And I can't explain why, but this makes me cry. A tear floats off my cheek with the zero gravity and circles the cabin like a baby Earth.

Landing minus one day

We close in on home. On life. On our people. The perfectly packed layers of atmosphere stretch out from Earth into the blackness of space beyond. It looks so flimsy, yet within it are all the shades of blue: furthest away an inky indigo holding the void at bay; closest to the surface a vivid cerulean, like sunlit water over the white Florida sand.

Sometimes even a scientist finds there just isn't enough poetry for the things she's seen.

And the thought occurs to me: *Shawn could have snitched days ago. He could have grounded me forever. But he didn't. He, too, chose to ignore the evidence.*

I'll tell him he was right to let me fly. After all, what is a mother without stories? If not for this blob, then for the sake of all future blobs I must go on exploring. And if this blob doesn't make it? Because it jumped, or was pushed? Well, one day both our particles – and maybe Shawn's too – will meet somewhere out here in the endless inky night, and mine will form into the shape of a giant arm and sweep across the cosmos as I say: 'You see? You see this, Blob? You'd have done the same thing as me, right?'

Right?

Landing minus six minutes

Fly into space all you want, you'll never fit in. You're a tourist, wearing your human mess around your neck like a camera. It's the mess that made you coo at the bloodless perfection of the universe in the first place, but it's the same mess that makes you want to fly back home again.

Soon there'll be mountains again. Then parking lots. Hornbeams. The roof of Shawn's building. Glass ashtrays filled with orange peel. A moth.

I could take all the tests. Maybe it'll be all right yet.

The ocean rushes upwards at us.

DORE KIESSELBACH

Non-Invasive

Deciding where to put you, my wife and I speak
of size we won't live to see.
It's the overhead wires we're concerned about.
We create space by killing what was there
with poison painted on ten breathing stumps,
amend a transition zone with peat
when the hole I dig reaches clay.
That they'll be ready to connect,
she roughs your roots up, the way
doubt cultivates us, while I hold you
by the slow persistence of your trunk.
In the corner of one eye I glimpse
a stranger sitting out in spring
when you're full grown
and do not envy him but wonder
what he thinks of what he sees.
Did we achieve our woodland paradise?
Putting you in is like stocking
a stream making a comeback
these years. Bending low to form
a raised soil circle for water
I'll pour each day around you for weeks,
my hands assume that basic shape
related to but more perfect than applause.

NICK MacKINNON

By Tompion and Banger

Today he came to take away the clock
that supervised my time between his sheets:
a month-duration longcase, made in London
by Tompion and Banger, with a square
twelve-inch face and Royal pendulum;
a slender crutch, a splayed and bevelled cock;
pierced blue steel hands; a glazed and hooded door;
the turban spandrels double screwed; the cleat's
brass leading edge punch-numbered 324;
the trunk hand-sorted walnut flame veneer
with delicately chased and gilt escutcheon.

Six months had intervened since he had gone;
six times she wound the clock, so its discreet
throat-clearing bongs could now divide the night
as once they parcelled out the afternoon,
when she would let the quarter's crisper ting
ring in the changes: now a steel-pierced tongue
would do the work of hands; now she would turn;
now arch; now loop her arms over the rail;
then by some Eighteenth Century miracle
the movement stops its chiming for a spell
till time begins again in tangled linen.

He left the cuckoo clock of course, a kitsch
Black Forest number made of MDF
and *vorsprung durch technik* Bavarian quartz,
whose 'parasite included' leitmotif
bounced off the kitchen's Corion and lino.
With *deus ex machina* timing (nicked

70

from Early Learning Centre's singalong
book-plus-cassette of *My Grandfather's Clock*)
the cuckoo went bananas as the men
carried the walnut longcase to their van.
It seemed it had been welshing tick and tock
from Tompion and Banger all along,
until an AA battery from the stash
beneath her bras and knickers fixed its mojo.

THIRD PRIZE

LYDIA FULLEYLOVE

Night Drive

So when the phone call came, saying
    that we should go back tonight, we were barely
surprised, we might have been waiting
    for it all our lives. We took two cars in case
it did not happen that night and one of us
    at least could drive home to sleep and I
followed my father so as not to lose my way
    through the twisting lanes in the dark
but I think it was marked in my head
    and I would not have faltered even
though all the time I was thinking
    of my mother, the bones stretching
her beautiful skin and her left eye almost
    closed, her face as clear as the rear lights
of my father's car or the sign of the inn
    where we'd eaten that morning.
There was nothing to do but to keep on
    driving, the car flowing between the banks
until at last we were crossing the glare
    of the town to the place where my mother
lay dying, though perhaps not tonight,
    we knew that the end might not be tonight.

JOSEPHINE ABBOTT

Iron Gall Ink

[*Ink used widely in medieval and later manuscripts, such as* Books of Hours, *Leonardo da Vinci's notebooks, the music MSS of J S Bach etc*]

What made me cry was not the simplicity of prayer
with all its middle ages *Oe*s and *Let me not*s;

not the carefulness of the minuscule script
it was written in, every angle and upstroke

pent with hours of backstrain, eyestrain;
not the sheer faith inhabiting the letters.

It was the story of the ink. The gall-wasp
pitting its sting against the oak tree; the acidic gall

growing round the poison; the slow strange
motion of all these things unknown, ongoing,

then, as now. What a harvest: ugly oak-sores
to mix with rusty-iron water. A chemistry

hardly understood, but an ink that lasts. Indelible.
Think of the prayers and patience of the makers.

Crush the galls and soak them for three days.
Then boil them in three quartes of rainwater

Oh the sadness of it. This ink – *encaustum* –
couldn't be scratched away; grew darker with age;

would've been permanent, except this slow writing
is eating away, like rust, the page it's written on.

LIZ BASSETT

No Place

The train's no place for a wean to sleep

not if she's carried on by her father
in her red plastic mac with the pink flowers
the heads heavy on their stems like summer;

not if he plants her hard on the floor
the smack of her plimsolls like a mug of tea
on to a table – twice, like a sour word

and the slapped face after —
the words tight fists with no air inside them:

      Staun.   Still.

              She's six at the most.
He shakes her like an envelope
for the tenner he knows won't be there;

peers at her like she's round a corner
or a queer dog someone brought to the pub.

I want to say something to make some of this better
— the shaking, the peering at her like she's a queer dog,
the holding her like an empty envelope —

I could say: *Let her sit here. She can sleep.*
She's no bother. But I don't speak

just watch her face, blank as a pebble,
her hands reaching for him over and over,
her fingernails like ten cold half moons.

No Place

When my friend had her daughter
she said her fingernails were so small
the only way to cut them was to bite them.

I imagine someone holding the girl's hands

first one   then the other

their breath like clouds across her fingers;
the slivers of moon new in their mouth.

ALAN BUCKLEY

Crimson

Your bed in the hospice looks out
over rows of cars, an embankment,
across which electric trains click

south and north, towards and away
from the coast. Jaundice has risen
up through you, as spilt tea rises

through a cube of sugar; the whites
of your eyes stained umber, your skin
like a brown paper bag, as liable,

it seems, to crease, or to crumple.
But when you slowly lift your head,
and gesture for us to embrace,

my gentleness - as I tuck my arms
beneath you, and brush one kiss
on your cheek - has nothing to do

with your frailty. There's a crimson
silk flower clipped in your hair. You
are a woman. You are not dead yet.

negative space

the cold winter night when neighbouring mother and son
ran to our Alberta door, when my father talked into the black
barrel of the drunken husband's hunting rifle

summer holidays when the most popular boy in high school,
student council president, caramel hair and rosewater skin
and just graduated with honours, hanged himself

the winter afternoon I was seventeen and the kid down our street
ran in front of my friend's car, the child's mother gathering, dabbing
a hand across bloodied blonde hair, tea towel raised against offers of help

the June midnight my grandmother who could not speak,
her mouth flaccid, pelvis bloated, would not die
until the rest of the family slept

the rainy night the wood and nails gave way the Kenyan bridge
one train after ours, washed two Canadian
tourists asleep in their bunks into the mouths of hippos

the Thanksgiving weekend my friend burned beside her husband
in the insect hull of a Cessna, while in the backseat
two young sons were scarlet seared

my babies whose hearts never moved
who remained grey and still and nameless
though for three months mustered form inside me

these missing spaces I could slip into –
into shadows, the bones and habits of a lover,
the catch of breath before morning.

CLARE DIPROSE

Mourning

I am eight again, and face my mother.
We grasp the corners of a sheet,
flick, crack and stretch white cotton
between us, match and straighten edges,
and walk to meet each other.

She passes me her corners,
slides her hands down, picks up the fold.
We back away until the fabric is taut,
begin again.   Dance it over and over.

What's left of the sun
slides down below the roof
and winter cabbages are shadowed with blue.
I fold cool pillowcases from the line,
drop inherited clothes-pegs
into my basket, one by one.
Low over the darkening hedge drifts
a pale nightdressed owl.

BEN HOLDEN

Relationship

I've watched you across this two by three metre bay-windowed room
      for several hours now
and you seem listless, unattended to, frankly: *stood up*.
      I'm basking
in the orange light passing through the broken blinds.
      You take to sitting upside
down, back on the bed, legs up the wall, your black sequined dress
      falls and pools
like a parachute sweetly to your head, revealing
      black underwear.
He really isn't coming – perhaps you just weren't his type.
      Perhaps he doesn't appreciate
that musk *we* like, its presence each wet daytrip
      or the finery
of sorts, I, your more proximate rescuer adorn you with:
      those crystal shining fibres
I've seen you pluck (after every hug).

I remember when we walked together through London
      one intoxicating peach-flecked dawn,
the wind was singing in the trees (the sound of atavistic
      bugle horns).
Who could have blamed me for cocking a leg
      and taking you home the longer route instead?
Now I rise, and you, seeing me, know this to be your cue.
      I can't help but be upset, though,
by your continuing posture up the wall.
      From the bed.
And I lie down, growling out the gloom
      he's put in both our heads.

RHIANNON HOOSON

Fictions

At night we'd tell each other stories:
In Egypt, we fed at the pomegranate's mouth
long notes of languor rose from the ground
falcons hovered at their tethers' farthest reach
and swam the air like fish.
Russia's long night moon stank of dust
and furs. Our fingertips
melted tiny clarities into the windows.
We remembered looking out at snow falling,
how the caesura panned to let owls rise
silent as soft wax before the night resumed.
Fictions are precise like this. We tracked
families back to their sources among cragged hills
where goats watched the births of children
with their pale eyes, and waited for the music
of whimpers that spilled from those left out
for the night to test. Somehow in winter
we came to the truth of it: how there were stars
once, formed from the hot weight
of a black other. How they hung
still and dark and raging and unknowable.
Nothing woke into the hot blankness of their reign
but we remembered them, and slept
fitfully, petty fictions sifting to dust
on the unswept floor, tangles of hair blown
beneath the bed, and the vastness of the stars only
inches above us, seeding silence
into the hot room.

CHRISTOPHER HORTON

Ultrasonic Mouse Deterrent

Listen. The mice are behind the skirting boards again
apparently immune to the special plugs we bought.
At least we lie above the pitch of ultrasonic screams
now riding the fug of left-out dhansak.
They are playing us for fools – making-out in the nooks,
tutoring their offspring on the strengths and weaknesses
of cereal packets, the entrances and exits of kitchen units,
the niche architecture of breadbins. Tell me,
how much of this ambience is amplified?
My arm rests on your hips,
simulates a gesture of sleep, but we are both pit-eyed,
staring at the curvature of furniture, none of it matching,
each piece a cut from our lives. And we are searching
for those bits in-between, the hunger we felt,
the things that won't come, not easily.
In this dirty-light, I am guessing too whether it is morning
or night, if the mice know we lie here, cogitating.
Feel how our bodies throb to the age-old beat
and are as warm as theirs.

HELEN OSWALD

Morning After

Sunday slicks in.
Unwoken by light
you lie in dreams.
Your bags are packed.

Romance is a parrot — .
I love you, I love you.
It parodies what cannot be put
into words, or cages.

Last night more was said
by the soft snow of parmesan,
a bright sprig of parsley
to freshen the breath.

Now we rock along the tracks.
The carriage draws
a thick line through this town.
Conversation sticks.

In Battersea, jailed dogs
yap at the quiet power station,
idling on its back,
legs to heaven.

At Victoria, a train door bangs shut.
The hard smack of sound hits us
and you slam on your smile
like a brake.

Hangover

Thrawn, athrob, heaved ashore by the only
breasts in the world – the sea's – it stood to reason
in a rock pool, learning, from a distance, its lesson;
sharks slicing up the bigger water looked lonely
from safety's clenched perspective, a Stanley
knife's fin-blade piercing blue corrugations
from beneath, opening, for all the world, a package of sky,
not water. Small crabs clung to the gravel like rations
pre-dropped for pick-up and a small flame danced
into a bigger one, tearing soft holes in the rockface.
The body showed soft holes too and sensitive tissue,
boils and haemorrhoids that had to be lanced;
back from the corner shop hid in the furze
came the bounding caveman with the latest issue.

ZACH FALCON

The Malamute

Joe Whitmore was a seiner out of Paul Harbor, Alaska. One summer morning he took his boat out alone and didn't come back. The Coast Guard found the *Glory B* days later, tied up clean at the transient float in Homer. A half mug of coffee sloshed gently on the galley table, atop a signed note that read in its entirety, 'Fuck You.' He left a wife and two children and a malamute dog in a log house set back in the woods above Mill Bay. No one in Paul Harbor ever heard from him again.

After the Coast Guard reported the boat found and apparently abandoned, a steady wash of rumour moved through the town. People sorting their mail at the tables in the post office or standing in line at Kraft's grocery tossed out dark theories: debt, infidelity, elaborate foul play. But few people knew Joe Whitmore well enough to go beyond idle speculation. He wasn't a highliner, and had been in the seine fleet for only six or seven years, not long by local standards.

The town knew even less about his wife, Meredith. From the Midwest somewhere, they thought. Some knew her in passing from the daughter being in school, but Meredith avoided parent activities and their guesses about her remained just that. She took a sewing class at the community college when they first moved to town. Someone recalled that she threw a fit when she couldn't get the plaid of a shirt to line up right. Tina Grogan had been there. 'A strange woman,' she commented later, hiking her eyebrows and shrugging her shoulders as though to indicate there was little more to say. 'Sort of stuck up. She seemed unhappy.'

After the Coast Guard found the boat and called off the search, the *Glory B*'s three crewmen parked on the road and walked up the trail to the cabin. The cabin sat on a rise in the woods, well back from the bluffs of the bay. The pulling ocean sounded faintly through the shadowed forest of spruce trees. The cabin was built with round logs, chinked with tar. It hadn't been maintained against the wet climate of Southwest Alaska. Black moss grew freely on the rotting logs; ditch grass sprouted on the shingles. A thick-billed raven hunched darkly on the roof ridge. It swiveled its attention to the men as they entered the clearing and then spread its wings from its chest and flew off, croaking.

The three crewmen climbed the worn half-log steps up to the listing porch. The skiffman, being older and experienced, led the delegation. The other two weren't more than boys. They found jobs on the *Glory B* by walking the docks two months before and were still green. One was drunk, having discovered nothing better to do while idle ashore.

The malamute dog lay on the threshold of the porch, watching the approach of the three warily. A large square dog, with near black eyes and white paws the size of a man's fist. His thick fur was burred with bits of devil's club and wrinkling green scraps of prickled salmonberry leaf. The drunk boy knelt and stroked the dog's broad muzzle, swaying slightly on his haunches as he did so. The dog's tail thumped once or twice against the porch but his wariness remained.

The skiffman stepped around the dog and knocked firmly on the plankwood door, scuffing the mud from his boots as he waited. The door had no provision for a lock, just a handle and a latch. After a moment the latch sprang and the pale face of a spindly girl peered out from the crack. She wore a blue crocheted poncho and pajama bottoms. She clutched a book of fairy stories to her chest.

'Is your dad home yet?' asked the skiffman.

The girl stared up at him without speaking and then shook her head a quick inch on either side, retreating as Meredith came to the door.

'What do you want?' Meredith asked. She was short, with dirty blonde hair cut in a bowl shape that framed her round face. She wore a bulky brown and white Icelandic sweater over a pair of jeans. She looked at the skiffman with red eyes, her expression slack and unfriendly.

'Came for our cheques,' said the skiffman. 'We fished half the season and are due to get paid.'

When she did not respond, he continued. 'I've got copies of the fish tickets and Joe's agreement on our crewshares right here if you want to see.' He dug beneath his orange raincoat and came out with a soiled manila envelope, scratched over with Joe's handwriting.

Meredith regarded the three men sourly, her eyes lingering for a moment on the drunk one. He was bent awkwardly at the waist with one hand in his jeans pocket and the other fumbling for a cigarette rolling away from him on the porch. She ignored the envelope.

'He owes you. I don't,' she said.

'We don't know where he is,' said the skiffman.

'Me neither.'

The skiffman exhaled and ran his tongue over his lower teeth. A boy came up behind Meredith, circling her around the leg with one arm, leaving the other hand free to pull on the end of a white piece of string he was chewing wetly in his mouth. The dingy toe-ends of his socks flapped as he shifted his small weight, eyeing the men.

'Noah, go and play with Grace,' she said sharply, brushing him back. The boy slunk out of sight into the dim stillness of the cabin.

'Look, Mrs. Whitmore,' said the skiffman when the boy was gone, 'we're owed a fair pot of money and we don't want to have to sue you for it.' The drunk nodded loosely behind him. The third crewman leaned against the porch rail, arms crossed.

Meredith snorted and turned down the corners of her mouth as if she had tasted something foul, her face contorting. 'Sue him,' she spat.

The skiffman flinched back as though struck. He still held the soiled envelope in his hand. He folded it along a worn crease and tucked it back into the belly pocket of his sweatshirt.

'Whatever,' he said finally, turning to leave. 'We'll be in touch.'

As the three men stomped down off the porch, Meredith stepped halfway out of the door. 'If you find that sonofabitch,' she yelled, 'tell him to come get his fucking dog.' She slammed the door. The sound echoed through the woods like a rifle shot.

Meredith leaned against the rough planking of the closed door for a moment and then walked to the kitchen table. She sat heavily, the legs of the chair scraping. Her breath convulsed, shuddering her body, and she wept. Grace stood at the picture window next to the stonework fireplace, watching the men leave the clearing and disappear into the trees as they followed the trail back to the road. Her eyes tracked the safety orange of the skiffman's slicker, winking brightly through the thicket of goat's beard and baneberry that encroached upon the clearing, until he disappeared in the darkness of the wood. Noah, with his flapping socks, stood mute between them in the heavy air of the cabin, chewing the string until the strands split against the roof of his mouth.

Meredith sat at the table all afternoon, staring blankly at the visible grain of its polished wood. Occasionally she'd remove a fraying wad of tissue from the sleeve of her sweater and wipe her nose, rocking softly against the back of the chair.

The children put themselves to bed, Grace nudging Noah along the newly abbreviated routine. They slept in the same room, small beds on either side of a window that opened to the back of the cabin, facing the inevitable junkyard of a commercial fisherman: piles of rotting seine web, engine parts, stacks of crab pots, coils of line, discarded kickers rusting half-hidden in the tall fireweed.

When the children were quiet, Meredith stood and filled a glass of water from the kitchen tap. It was well water, pungent and coloured rust with iron. She drank it down and filled it again, drinking the second glass quickly, eyes fixed and blank, her breath gulping and laboured from the effort. She set the glass on the counter and walked to the door. The latch stuck slightly, from having been slammed.

On the porch she pulled on her boots. She did not look at the dog, who curled his head toward her with benign interest. She stomped her feet into the boots as she strode to the back of the porch, where it was level with the ground, and began picking through the junk behind the cabin.

She found a section of rebar that Joe had bent into a right angle to reinforce the corner of a crab pot, and a yellow coil of stiff braided nylon line. She carried them both to an open patch of ground between the trees just beyond the clearing. She pushed the ends of the rebar into the soil as far as she could and then walked around to the woodpile in front of the cabin, returning to the open patch with the axe dragging behind her.

She pounded the rebar into the ground with the butt of the axe-head, holding it tight like a hammer at first and then swinging it full, the wood of the handle neck splintering against the steel bar when she missed.

With the rebar stuck firm in the ground, only a shallow triangle showing above the dirt, she fixed one end of the rope to it with a lopsided series of square knots. She tugged against it to test, leaning back with her weight. Then she dropped the rope end and walked back to the porch.

The dog was sleeping at the threshold of the door, and blinked at Meredith groggily when she stood over him.

'Get up,' she said.

The dog raised his head, but did not otherwise stir. Meredith gripped the dog by the fur of his neck and pulled him sharply upright. The dog stood, confused, and shook himself. She lost her grip when he shook so she took him again and pulled him along the porch to the open space. The dog balked at first, nails scratching on the porch, and then trotted alongside willingly as though invited to a game beyond his devising.

She took the free rope end and tied a collar around the dog's neck, tying the same series of square knots as on the rebar. Then she turned back to the house. The dog started to follow but heaved up short when the line went taut. The dog watched her intently, ears forward, as she stepped up onto the porch and re-entered the cabin.

Meredith came back onto the porch with a half-full bag of dog food hoisted on her shoulder, the sack-paper crinkling in her ear. She carried it down the log steps and set off on the trail to the road. It was well into evening, near eleven o'clock, but the sky was still light and she knew the path well enough that even amidst the gloom of the trees she did not stumble. The path led around red gnarls of tree root and was bordered for a stretch with white clam shells and sea glass collected and arranged by Grace the year before.She came out of the trees and stepped up the loose grade to the gravel road. Joe's blue pick-up sat parked on a potholed apron near the trail. Meredith dumped the bag of dog food into the back of the truck. It landed heavily, spilling brown marbles of kibble loose into the wet wales of the truck bed. She wiped her hands on her jeans and turned back to the cabin. Through the trees she could hear the dog already barking.

Meredith slept that night in her clothes, after first pulling shut the heavy drapes against the uncanny blue twilight that lingered until dawn. Noah's hand pushing on her shoulder roused her awake. He stood next to the bed in his pyjamas, working a bent thumb into his nose absentmindedly.

'It's morning,' he said. 'How come Jonas is tied up?'

Meredith blinked at him, as though he were a stranger. There were red welts on her face where she had slept on her sweater, twisting in the night. The boy was breathing loudly through his mouth as he continued working the thumb.

'He's sick,' she said. 'Don't go near him.'

'But he's barking a lot.'

'Because he's sick. You and Grace just leave him alone, okay?'

Noah nodded slowly, breathing.

'Please stop picking your nose.'

He removed his thumb and examined it briefly. 'How come you're wearing all your clothes?'

'Because I'm feeling sick, too. Both of you just need to leave me alone.'

Meredith rolled away and pulled the blanket to her face. Noah stood for a few minutes, shifting his weight from foot to foot tentative and uncertain, then shuffled out of the dark room, closing the door behind him.

For the next two days Meredith rarely left her bed. The dog barked and howled without cease. The children watched the dog from the edge of the clearing, not daring to approach. The dog lunged wildly against the rope, running like a compass-pencil at the extent of the tether, inscribing a bitter circle in the earth. At times the dog would drop, panting, into a crouch. The rope was burning away the thick fur of the dog's neck, exposing a rust-coloured ring of scored flesh.

'Do you wanna go throw rocks?' asked Noah.

Grace shook her head slowly, not looking at him, transfixed by the dog.

Noah shrugged and wandered away slack-jawed, picking his nose. He gathered a pocketful of gravel and squatted next to the well, some thirty paces from the front of the cabin, down a gentle slope. The well was four-foot square at the surface, a deep hole with heavy black visqueen sheathing the sides. A short timber frame anchored the plastic and supported the scrap plywood cover. Noah shoved a corner of the cover back and shivered at the dank cold air that escaped. The water was two feet below the opening, dark and scummed with spruce needles. Noah dropped his collection of stones into the well one at a time, listening intently to each splash, like a catch of breath, as they fell.

When he ran out of rocks, Noah found a toy that his father had given him forgotten in the growing weeds under the porch. A heavy Kong ape figure, rubbery and filled with gel allowing its limbs to stretch when pulled. Noah took the doll to the woodpile and dismembered it on the chopping block, striking it intently with the hatchet. The red gel oozed forth onto the block and smeared the hatchet's pitted blade. Noah gathered up the pieces and threw them into the well, committing them to the water.

On the third or fourth day of steady barking, Pete Dombrowski, a neighbour to the north through the woods, knocked on the door. He and his wife had been guests once or twice at dinner. He'd played cribbage with Joe over coffee and brandy, and had figured what was coming. He wasn't surprised when it did. But he didn't gossip and had kept his mouth shut at the post office while others speculated.

Meredith opened the door and greeted him with a mumble.

'Just checking in, hey,' said Pete, tall and grinning, holding out a package the size of a bread loaf wrapped in brown butcher paper. 'Some halibut for you guys. Caught it yesterday. It'll freeze just like this if you've no call for it in the next few days.'

Meredith made no move to take it. 'We're okay,' she said.

'Oh, sure you are,' said Pete. 'We just had some extra. Caught it on sport gear, hey. Can't sell it.' He thrust the package toward her and she took it reluctantly.

'So you're fine?'

'We're fine.'

'Good, hey.' Pete smiled and nodded. 'Give me or Rose a call if you need anything. Anything at all.'

Meredith nodded and closed the door. Pete stood for a moment and then walked to the back edge of the porch, rubbing his hands together, chill from carrying the halibut. His face flattened as he watched the dog, crouched in the dirt, panting heavily. Pete spit and walked home through the trees.

Meredith dropped the package on the kitchen table and sat with her hands clutched white in her lap, staring into the middle distance. Grace approached carefully, placing her fingertips on the edge of the table as though addressing a piano.

'Why can't we feed Jonas?' she asked.

'If your father wants to feed him, he can.'

'But . . .'

Meredith slapped her palm flat on the table hard. Grace jumped back, hiding her fingers in protective fists. The noise burst in the kitchen then faded, ringing in the air. Meredith stared down at the table and spoke evenly, with a high edge to her voice, emphasizing every word. 'I'm doing the best that I can,' she said. 'I'm doing the best I can.' She sniffled and pulled the gray wad of tissue from her sleeve. Grace stepped away, unnoticed, not turning her back until she had reached the living room.

That afternoon the electric pump in the well quit and they had to carry water buckets for washing and flushing the toilet. Meredith lost her temper at the sputtering faucets, slamming the cabinets and stomping on her heels as she walked, fuming. Noah grew sullen, fretting guiltily around the mouth of the well, staring into black depths where the contraption had surely jammed on his ravaged toy.

While the children hauled the splashing buckets of brown water up from the well, Meredith calmed and seemed to rally. She busied herself in the kitchen, cooking some of the halibut and baking a batch of oatmeal cookies, which Grace especially admired. They sat at the table with only three chairs. Meredith lit a candle stub to place between them and hummed while she served the dinner. The children ate quietly, forks tapping against the plates. Meredith smiled broadly at them both and proposed a toast to adventure. 'Everything new begins from now on,' she said. The hoarse voice of the dog continued to sound outside.

Noah ate steadily, but Grace picked at her food. When Meredith went to the bathroom, Grace's plate was still full. Grace waited until the bathroom door closed and then she stood, holding her plate before her carefully, and went outside. Noah watched her unlatch the door and step onto the porch.

'Mom,' he called. 'Mom! Grace is feeding Jonas.' Meredith ran from the bathroom, jeans unzipped, and stormed onto the porch. Noah heard yelling, and the sound the of the plate breaking. Meredith swept back into the house wrenching Grace by the arm, dragging her to the bedroom. The door slammed. The silverware on the table jumped. There were muffled cries.

Noah sat alone at the table, swinging his legs and eating through the stack of cookies. He chewed, letting the crumbs flake onto his lap, as the candle guttered down into its socket, casting lurching shadows against the walls.

They awoke the next morning to silence and found the dog gone. The rust-coloured collar of rope lay empty in the dirt, pulled free in the night. Over the next few days, the children would occasionally see the dog coursing through the woods, skinny and wild. Grace called when she saw him, but the dog did not turn or slow. He howled in the night, demoralized and haunted. Neighbours found their rabbit hutches tipped and their yards torn with blood and fur. Someone came across a deer mauled in the thicket. A Labrador was killed.

Meredith took a job at the cannery, working long hours on the slime line and picking shrimp with taciturn Filipino women for overtime. When she came home to fall into exhausted sleep, the children would retch at the gutty stench of her clothes.

Grace was left in charge of Noah during the day, but she refused to speak with him. Only once did she acknowledge him at all.

'Do you wanna throw rocks?' he asked.

Grace looked at him square. 'You bastard,' she said.

He shuffled away, thumb working in his nose, and neither spoke further.

One afternoon, Grace sat idle on the chopping block, reading her book of stories and picking at splinters, when she saw Pete Dombrowski step into the clearing. He walked slowly and had a black-barrelled deer rifle slung on a leather strap on his shoulder. Grace regarded him with alarm, standing barefoot in the scattered wood chips.

'What are you doing?' she asked.

'Nothing sweetheart,' said Pete, shaking his head. 'Just going for a walk.'

'I know . . .' said Grace. 'I know what you are doing.'

Pete stopped and looked at her and nodded once. 'Then you should go inside.'

Grace clutched at her patchwork skirt and stared at Pete intently. 'We're not okay,' she said with rising panic in her voice. 'We're not okay.'

Pete swallowed and pressed his lips together. 'I know, kiddo,' he said. 'I know that.' He stared at her for a moment longer, then turned and stalked slowly out of the clearing, threading his way noiselessly through the trees.

An hour or so later a shot rang out sharply in the distance, then another, then silence. Noah was squatting at the lip of the well. He stood at the noise and looked toward Grace, standing on the porch. He saw her face go white then crumple redly before she turned and went inside.

Noah squatted again. Floating below on the surface of the well were the remnants of the Kong doll. The heavy gel had dissolved, leaving the cut pieces of rubber to rise to the surface. Noah fished at them with a length of spruce branch, hooking one, a leg, which he buried in a roothole. He swiped at the others as they bobbed out of reach, sinking under. He leaned, stretching forward over the dark water with the stick, bracing his leg against the wooden lip of the well. A rotted section gave way, the board slapping flat against the ground as it pulled from the nails. Noah pitched thrashing into the water, gripping the spruce branch tightly in his fist. The branch stiffened against the wall as he fell and the jagged end in his hand pushed sharply into his face. He felt a searing pain and tried to scream but he was beneath the water. He thrashed and scrabbled until his head was clear and then he screamed and screamed.

That night, after the hospital, after the yelling and the crying, when the cabin was dark and silent, Noah lay in his bed feverish and in pain. A white gauze patch was taped hugely over his left eye, and orange iodine smears covered the scratches on his face and arms. Grace lay awake in her bed nearby, listening to his ragged and whimpering breath. She set aside her book of stories and slid from beneath the blankets. She crawled next to him, wrapping her spindly arms around him firm and gentle, rocking him in the dark.

'Shh,' she said, 'shhh.'

'Oh god,' said Noah, gulping. 'It hurts it hurts it hurts.'

'Hush now,' soothed Grace, petting him.

Noah shook and whimpered in her arms. She whispered in his ear. 'You must be strong. You are a pirate now. You will wear a patch and sail the pirate seas. You are like Odin now. Hush.'

Outside the wind rose in the night, creaking the darkening wood that grew ever closer upon the cabin. The children held each other, centered in the darkness at the edge of the world. The wind howled. A haunted sound, moaning through the trees.

HELEN GEOGHEGAN

The War Baby

I am at the river when I see him. I am fourteen years old and I am about to become a liar. The only reason I keep looking is because of his clothes. I never saw a man's coat so soft. My father's clothes are just for wearing.

When he starts talking to me he loosens his tie a bit. I think this is quite a nice thing to do. It makes me feel shy. His shirt is the kind of blue I thought only girls wore. He has silver bands round his shirt sleeves and earrings instead of buttons at the wrist. He puts one hand in his trouser pocket, the trousers have pleats. The way he does this, you can tell he's careful with himself. I want to smooth myself down. I wish I had a ring or a necklace. Touching my skirt I find the back has moved around to the front. I tug it hard when he's not looking so my clothes face the right direction again.

I don't know what we say but I finish sentences that surprise me. I feel parts of me stick out when he looks at me as if he knows me already. When I'm speaking to him I think that my eyes and the corners of my face are very interesting.

Two mornings later I meet him on the way to school. My sister revs up her agitation like an engine then marches on. For her, there's only one pathway through the day.

We begin to go for walks together. He's either funny in a way that makes me feel smart or something like sad. I don't know the word for it. We don't have that kind of sadness at home.

He can tell what the weather will be by looking at the sky and he has names for all the fields. He goes for a walk by himself when the dew is spread, pulls the button head mushrooms and fries them for his breakfast after mass. He says one day we will do that together. He says it as if it's like getting married.

If we meet people he smiles and says 'looks like the rain', even if it's sunny. He tells me stories about his travels. In London, they don't put enough salt in the bread but in Italy they do. He tells me where the fairy forts are in the fields. The fairies gather there after six and he knows how

94

to follow their trail. He says that we can't hear their words because we have the wrong kind of ears. They are very powerful and can even kill dogs and cows just with their eyes.

I talk too; I say things I never heard before and he just nods his head as if he knew what I was going to say. When we're walking he touches my arm if he's going to stop and explain something; after three times this really annoys me. One time he touches my arm to pull me to a stop. He pauses like a priest then says 'It will be difficult for you.' I know it will be difficult for me if he keeps doing that.

Then I start going to his old stone house and making more secrets. Most of the tall rooms are completely empty, the doors half closed as if they want no dealings with each other. The rooms are for standing things in, not for doing things. His bicycle leans in the front room against a mantelpiece. In another room, a painting with a broken frame stands on a single chair. The painting shows the side of a woman's face and her neck. Even though I can't see all of her, I can tell she's not happy. She looks like someone forgot her. While I look at her, he stands in the doorway. His head nearly reaches the top. He says 'you need a good coat.' He's a big one for coats.

The hall you step into from the street is paved in cold flagstones. It runs down to the kitchen which has a square sink underneath a bare dirty window. The dirt is old-fashioned. A table, shoved against the wall, is covered in flowered linoleum. On the table there's the constant confetti of breadcrumbs. The breadboard, the tin of mustard, the big knife, and the two eggcups are never moved from the table. We have our tea together. He leaves a bag with a cream donut on the table. It's the first thing I look for when I come; there's always a small sheet of cellophane stuck on top of the cream. I wonder if I didn't come, would he eat it.

He ties a shirt around his waist like an apron. Our tea is always the same: cheese, hard and orange, a boiled egg and white batch bread with a black chewy crust. The tea we drink is tormented with tea leaves. They don't seem to bother him but mine go astray and get stuck in the roof of my mouth, like a warning. My granny has a strainer. You'd think someone with bracelets for his shirt and earrings for his buttonholes would get a strainer.

When I saw his clothes I thought he'd have carpets and glass bowls. But the first time I go inside the house I am disappointed. Everything is tired and used up. I think I might not want to go for a walk with him again. But then we have our tea and we're talking when something happens. We both stop making sentences, we just sit there and part of me stops in a rest; a part I didn't even know was tired. Then I forget about the broken house like he does.

After my cream donut, I swallow the tea as quickly as I can. But one tea leaf always sticks. That one tea leaf tells me I will be in trouble — for resting a part of me here with the man — for knowing things without anybody telling me — for eating cakes and telling lies. When we are finished and the mustard is drying in the egg cup he wipes the linoleum adding a layer of water to the breadcrumbs. Then we go to his room where the fire is already lit. I sit on my hands while he gets ready. First he has his pipe then he stands up and opens his belt. He coughs a bit to loosen his voice. Then he begins, to sing his sadness into me....

'Lay your head upon my pillow, hold your warm and tender body close to mine.

Hear the whisper of the raindrops blowing soft across the window.

And make believe you love me one more time. For the good times.'

The lumpy thing in his throat moves. His jaws are a bit shaky and his eyes seem like they're pleading with the window. He closes them when his thick voice creeps up my back. I don't know if he does this to remember or to forget. As the melody picks its way through me it forms a frequency for this sound. This is the sound of love and the sound of love is sad. Later, whenever I hear that song, my body responds with its own recording which is stuck so deep inside me I can't turn it off. I don't know if he's trying to catch or let something go with his song. I lie on the candlewick bedspread curled toward the window wishing the drops of rain could hit my face. He sings it at the window but he's singing it at me, at my girl's body and my young heart. And as I feel his curdled love, I feel his sadness grip my throat. It fills with hard little pellets I can't swallow. All of the space in me is filled up.

This is how love leaves its recording in my body. But it was too old for me. It's what was lost in him, pushing its way through me.

He feels better after. I know because he bangs his pipe on the hearth, then presses fresh tobacco into it. He lights it and the smell begins to crawl over me. I feel heavy, like I've forgotten how to move myself. It feels like there's a nail stuck in the back of my neck. So I just lie there and watch him glow when he sucks on the pipe. Then he tells me a story and I begin to empty.

I don't have to go back- no one makes me — but I want something. I don't know what. I don't know how to turn around into the way it was before.

Whenever I see him down the town he ignores me, even if I've had my tea with him the evening before. He's good at it. He smiles and talks to people and touches his hat. But sometimes it does my head in. I want to go up to him and say 'will you buy me a cake?' But other times I come out of school and he's outside the sweet shop and his face is terrible. He looks like he's just woken from a bad dream. Even in his nice clothes he looks frightened. He doesn't cross the road or say anything; he just looks at my face like he's trying to find something. We never made up these rules. I wonder how we both know them, maybe because I'm a natural liar. My brother sees me closing his front door. He doesn't wave. He just stares and then ignores me when I get home.

One day, he asks me to go to Dublin. I meet him at the bus station; he smells sweet and sticky. He is wearing his fancy navy coat; the one with letters stitched inside. All I have is my sister's cardigan, it's blue and there's a hole in the sleeve for sticking your finger in. I keep putting the cardigan on and taking it off. I don't know whether I want to be covered up or free. While we wait, he gives me a parcel. It's not big enough to hold a coat. We go on a bus. I get sick. We get off at some town which isn't even half way to Dublin. I am sorry that it's going wrong. I watch girls going into a convent. I am looking at the statue of Our Lady just inside the gate; it has a hand missing. He is looking at me again. I can always feel when he's doing it. I don't mind. In my house you get checked over quickly when you go in the door but they'd never look at you for no reason.

'What you need...' he says to me, 'is soda water'.

We go into a hotel. It's brown and still with so many layers of smells that you might forget things. I never had soda water before and I'm disappointed. He drinks whiskey. We don't talk. He buys another fat glass of whiskey while I open my parcel. I hold the brown gloves which have a smell. They feel soft like material but he says they're leather. Before putting the gloves on me, he takes hold of my hand. Then he turns it over and traces his finger along the inside of my wrist. When he does this, the world goes very small. It's quite nice but it doesn't make him happy. I get the feeling he's been in a very bad accident.

I try to get comfortable in the leather chair but it feels sticky next to my skin. I slide my leather hands under my legs to keep them off the chair. I wish I didn't feel sick so I could get chocolate and peanuts. That's what I get when my father brings my brother and me to the real pub. Sitting here with him is very different than sitting in his kitchen. I don't really want anything and I don't like that. I know that I have let him down but I feel so sick, I don't care. I feel like the dark musty room is swallowing up some of my life. If anyone saw me sitting there they wouldn't know I had brothers and sisters and a broken plate under my bed. Very suddenly, I miss the kitchen and I miss my brother's hair. I even miss his marbles. I am worried I will be stuck with pipes and man things forever.

We have to wait a long time for the bus home. The waiting is full of measurements. I am measuring how far it is to him and how far back to somewhere else. I don't know what he's measuring but he's measuring something. I always know when people are doing it, even though they never do it out loud. We are far away from each other. He unwraps a Milky Mint and puts it in his mouth. He doesn't offer me one even though he knows I like them. I don't ask because I am keeping the separateness. I have to be in a lot more places than him, which I think annoys him. But he gets to be the same person in the same place all the time. I only do this sometimes — when the silence he puts between us isn't a rest but a punishment.

At the station I feel bad to leave him sad.

I am catching his sadness.

I am also relieved.

One feeling lies down in my chest and just when I know what it is, a different one lies down beside it. Neither of us says anything about when we will have tea. The way we leave each other is always jerky; like we don't know how to do it. Walking away, I take off the cardigan and gloves. Then I turn around and look at him but I don't know what I see. I see his legs striding under his coat and his hard, shiny shoes. I see his jaw, where he holds his plans and promises, but it's crooked. It looks ugly. I don't know what it says.

I go home and tell more lies. I didn't know I'd be such a good liar. My sister bangs the door when she leaves the kitchen. Later, in bed she holds herself so hard we don't touch. I miss her. I didn't know that being allowed to touch someone was that important.

Eating batch bread in the stone house, he lectures me about health; mostly lungs. He knows a lot about health. I have bad dreams about lungs strangling me. He talks about T.B. for three tea times and sanatoriums — where you go when you have it. I prefer him talking about fairies. They know things; they don't ever not know.

He has handkerchiefs embroidered with his three initials. That's because he was a war baby and when he came here during the war, his initials were stitched inside all his baby clothes. It's a very special thing to have done on your behalf; maybe that's why he's kept it up. I've seen programmes about air-raid shelters and sirens during the war. I try to imagine him as a baby, bundled up in special embroidery; being carried through the bombs — his marshmallow skin and soft dopey eyes. I wish that had happened to me.

He gets sick. When I go there at tea time, I go up to his room and sit with him. I get no cakes. His skin is the colour of stones. Since we went on the bus he's not the same. He's missing something; like his rooms. There are flecks of blood in his eyes like red ink. With his head sideways on the pillow he looks different. He tells me about Scarlet O'Hara, from the film; he's mad about her. She made a dress out of a pair of curtains, saved her father's land and threw herself down a staircase because of a man. He says she had style. He teaches me some of the lines. His favourite is: 'I reckon that's your misfortune my dear, I don't give a damn.' He says this so many times I get annoyed and remind him that he's sick.

His house is cold. His good clothes are thrown over the chair like a dummy. I get the digestive biscuits and stick them together with butter. He doesn't want any. I mean to leave him some but then I eat them all. He goes into a hospital where they have paid nuns. The nuns there don't smell like the ones I'm used to but they don't go out so they can't tell anyone about me.

I find Scarlet O'Hara's face on a postcard and write something on the back. The day I pass his house and take it to the hospital, there's cold sleety rain. I have to swallow a lot before I go in. I move the small plastic crucifix and prop Scarlet up where they can see each other. Her brazen eyes watch him dying. I know that's what he's doing even though I haven't seen it before. We make jokes about the nun's clothes and their flour faces. We say nothing about after; when he won't be in his house. I put on his peaked hat. I say things that are so funny I nearly start crying. It hurts him to laugh but he tries then he has to turn away to spit in a bowl. I take the crucifix and put it in my jacket. I don't give him a hug. I turn my face so he can look at it. It's his last chance to find whatever it is he's been looking for. He says something to me and I forget it straight away. None of his words will be found in my mouth.

The sleet hurts my face when I walk away from the hospital. I am afraid of what people might see. I am worried that something will be shown that cannot be understood or put back. My back has splinters in it and I can't move my neck. All from making up lies in the cold.

My sister's the only one who looks up when I go into the kitchen. She's the one who sets a bit of herself aside when I'm not there. A part of her face is shut. That is my punishment. I am glad to be in the noisy house for tea time where there are no wet crumbs or tea leaves. I make stains on the soda bread with the beetroot and imagine the partitions inside me. I hope no more will form. They make me tired.

At dinner time the next day my father says: 'Clancy is dead — the Englishman.'

I'm not used to hearing his name, never mind the other word he puts after it.

'Who's that?' says my mother in the voice she uses for the weather. She doesn't care about the weather.

'You know, lived in the big stone house, striking man.'

Nothing happens to my face. I walk back to school with my sister's long legs as she tries to leave me behind.

When my father puts on his coat in the evening he doesn't say he's going to clear his head so I ask him where he's going. You're not allowed to sneak out of our house.

'Thought I'd go to Clancy's mass,' he says. 'He's got no-one.'

'Can I come?'

'There won't be any stopping in the shop on the way back' he says.

Then I know it is ok to go. He thinks I am the same girl I was before.

His coffin is open. My father blesses himself over the yellow face that I don't know. I stand there not looking down but watching the others to see if they can see anything on my face. To see if something started leaking. Because it's an early Easter there's a crucifix wrapped in a purple cloth. It's cradled just like a doll in a pram. My mother doesn't like purple but she says you should always pay attention to the cross. In my mind I try to sing his song about the sad rain on the window, but it doesn't work.

After, I don't know what to do. I try to avoid my brother's beady little eyes. I get into bed and play with the cross because there's a knot in me. I'm not crying when my sister gets into bed. I am pressing my stomach hard into the pillow to stop something. She moves her bare leg right over until it finds mine; this means I'm forgiven. I wake tangled up in her.

I go to the hospital to give the cross back. It's warm in my pocket. 'I picked this up by mistake' that's what I'll say. Because I've no-one to visit, I have to wait in the room with the four smells. The slow nun comes in with a plastic bag. She holds it out like it might dirty her dress and says 'Your friend left this for you.' I leave the cross in my pocket and take the faded plastic bag. Inside are Scarlet's face and his peaked hat which smells of pipe. I frame the tired postcard covering what is written on the back. Now Scarlet watches me. I'm not dying. I'm doing something else.

Later, I find the word for what he had. I find it in a dictionary my father gave me. It's called desolation. Not the tuberculosis, the other thing.

KATE HENDRY

Don't Say Anything

Dad wouldn't come to the house. He would park by Savory's and wait there. It would be better if Gordon and Annie walked up to meet him. 'Your mother,' he reminded Annie when he rang to arrange. It was because of Mum that he couldn't pick them up.

Mum had been angry when Annie had told her. 'You will wait for him here,' she had declared. She'd been angry all that evening and the rest of the weekend. By Monday morning she had calmed down and had seemed normal all week, though she hadn't mentioned it once and that wasn't like her. Then the night before, she got all sad and came upstairs to help Annie pack. It was the first time she and Gordon had stayed overnight with Dad. He hadn't had room for them before. This was his new flat, he'd got it specially so he'd have space for them. Mum folded Annie's clothes carefully so they wouldn't crease, even her knickers.

'I'm going to miss you so much,' she said, patting down her nightie.

She'd miss their Saturday night in front of the telly with a takeaway from the chippy. Annie's fish cakes, Mum's scampi. Mum would have beans on toast instead.

But in the morning, Mum didn't come up for her. She shouted from the bottom of the stairs for Annie to get up.

'You'll miss your appointment with your father.'

Normally she knocked on Annie's door and then came in, right up to her bed to wake her up. Annie didn't need her there of course, she could get up on her own. It was a habit they'd got into, what they'd always done.

Another thing was different. When Annie got downstairs, bumping her bag behind her, Mum was already dressed. Mum was never dressed before breakfast. She was wearing work clothes, even though it was Saturday. A skirt with a split up the back and a green jacket with shoulder pads and a pinched-in waist and lots of buttons.

Gordon gave Annie a look when she came into the kitchen. A don't-say-anything look. Mum had her back to them, she had the bread under the grill. It was burning. Someone had to speak.

'Mum, the toast,' said Gordon.

And that was all it took.

'Here,' she yelled, throwing toast at them both, 'take it with you, I'm sure you can't wait to leave.'

Annie picked up some pieces of toast from the back door mat.

'Better still,' Mum yanked the bin out of the cupboard under the sink, 'throw them away.' She rattled the bin under their faces. 'Go on, throw them away. Get your father to feed you, that's what you want isn't it? I'm sure he'll do it brilliantly.' She thrust the bin at them so that it fell against their legs and the insides came out.

There were tea bags and dried up spaghetti and empty dog-food tins all over the floor. It was nearly 10 o'clock already. That was when they were supposed to meet Dad.

'You get your coat,' said Gordon, 'I'll clear up.'

He got the dustpan and brush out. Annie went for her coat and shoes. She could hear Mum crying in the bathroom.

'We have to go,' said Gordon, following her into the hall.

'What about Mum?'

Gordon called out, 'we're off now, see you later,' as if they were leaving for school.

Annie looked up the stairs. She wanted to go up, she wanted a proper goodbye, but she didn't want Dad to have to wait. He hated having to wait.

'Bye Mum,' she called, her voice didn't seem loud enough.

Mum came to the top of the stairs and looked down at them. She wasn't crying.

'If you go now, don't come back,' she said it slowly, not shouting.

'Just ignore her,' Gordon whispered, 'she doesn't mean it.'

They had to go, leaving it like that. Mum stayed at the top of the stairs. Annie knew she was watching them.

Dad was already there. He was standing with his back to them, hands in his pockets rattling his change, looking up the High Street. Gordon called out to him as they got closer. He turned round and opened his arms for Annie to run into. Gordon was too old for that kind of thing. It was hard to run when she was carrying her bag and it seemed to take ages to get to him. Dad hugged her and lifted her feet off the ground. She was still holding onto her bag. It got in Annie's way when she tried to stand upright again.

Everything alright?' asked Dad, looking at Gordon.

'Mum's in a huff,' said Gordon.

'Oh dear,' said Dad in a way that sounded like he wasn't surprised. 'That's your mother for you.'

He opened the car door for Annie, then went round to the front.

'Cheer up,' he said, looking at her through his driver mirror, 'you're with me now.'

Annie tried to smile. She wanted to say that Mum wouldn't have been in a huff if it hadn't been for him. But she couldn't say it, hurt him more than he'd already been. He'd cried when he lost the custody battle. Mum had seen it. She said it was the only time she'd ever seen him cry. She'd given him joint custody then, because she felt sorry for him. Not that it meant much, just that he had a right to see them, with the law on his side. And he could pick them up wherever he said.

Dad's flat was in St Andrew's Road, not far from the university. It was number 1, so it was on the corner. Lots of buses went past and there was a bus stop practically on the doorstep. He could hop on the 35, 46 or 71 and be in the city centre in 10 minutes he said. Right in the heart of things.

The flat was in the basement. Dad said the ones further up the building were too expensive. He was only renting, but still, it was a lot of money, especially with the extra bedroom for them to stay. A bed-sit, if it had been just him, would have been much cheaper.

The main door was for all the flats. As they went in someone was going up the stairs. A man with jeans on and only a vest on top. They couldn't see his face. In the hall there was a huge cupboard. Letters were piled on top. Dad checked to see if there were any for him. He showed them the inside of the cupboard, it was full of envelopes.

'For all the people that used to live here,' said Dad, 'they move out and don't come back for their mail. Nobody knows where they've gone.'

Annie wanted to sort them into piles, in case they came back. What if there was an urgent message? But she wanted to get into Dad's flat too, in case anyone else came down stairs, or through the front door and caught them standing in the hallway.

They had to go down some dark stairs to get to Dad's front door.

'The flat's a bit damp,' Dad warned, 'no one's lived here for a while.'

Annie wondered where the last person had gone. Maybe, if they'd moved out years ago that was all their mail upstairs.

The damp smell was worst in the hall. It had orange walls.

The living room had windows looking out onto a small courtyard and a wall. It had a sofa and the green velvet chair that was Dad's, that he'd always sat in at home. Mum had let him have it. There was no TV. Dad wasn't going to get one.

'I'm not sharing with Annie,' said Gordon as soon as Dad showed them the spare room.

'It's alright,' said Dad, pulling Annie into him, 'she can come in with me.'

He took Annie back across the hall to his room.

'Teenage boys,' he said, 'smelly creatures, you wouldn't want to share with him anyway. And I promise not to snore.'

Dad had bought a brand-new double bed in the sales. He'd got a king size for the price of an ordinary double.

'Plenty of room for the two of us,' he told Annie.

The pavement came halfway down the window, with a grille to let in light. Sometimes feet walked over it and made it clang.

Dad took them to the Observatory, so they could see the city.

'It's your city now,' he told them, 'your home too.'

If Dad wanted it to be their city, maybe that meant he was staying. Annie checked to see if Gordon was going to say something sarcastic, but he was looking pleased. Almost smiling, even. He hated Ashbury now, he was always going on about how provincial it was. Bourgeois, he said. It was his new word. There weren't any communists in Ashbury. And all the pubs knew he wasn't 18 yet.

There were 93 steps to climb up to get to the top of the Observatory. They were shut into a dark room with other people. In the middle was a huge white saucer. You could see roofs and roads, houses and moving blobs. Dad said they were cars. The fuzzy shapes were trees. They tried to work out where Dad's flat was, but the picture was too hazy. The clouds stopped it working properly.

When they got down Dad said they could walk across the suspension bridge, stand in the middle to look down the river. It was cold and windy in the middle but at least they could see more of the city from there. Dad was pleased because it was only 2p each. The tide was out and there was hardly any water in the river, just smooth brown mud creeping up the banks.

Annie wanted to phone Mum when they got back to the flat. She'd left it so late already. Mum would want to know she was safe and sound. But

Dad didn't have a phone, he wanted to save on his bills. There was a pay phone in the hall. Annie didn't want to go up there, to the hall, on her own. She couldn't disappear up there, without saying to Dad. She didn't want to ask, to bring the subject of Mum up. Maybe she could get Gordon to phone.

'What for?' he said, 'we'll be home tomorrow. And she'll just shout anyway. No thanks.'

Annie didn't want to get shouted at either, but it would be worse if they didn't.

'I haven't got any coins,' said Annie, 'only a five-pound note.'

Gordon shrugged. They were in the living room while Dad was in the kitchen making the tea. Gordon was bored without the TV, he had nothing to do.

'She might not be so angry tomorrow if we phone tonight,' said Annie.

'Ask Dad for some money then,' he knew Annie was right.

'You,' Annie hated him. He always made things so hard.

'You're such a wimp,' said Gordon, pulling himself out of the sofa.

He came back with Dad.

'You should have reminded me,' said Dad, drying his hands on a tea towel. He had a jar of 10ps. 'I'll come up with you.'

Annie looked at Gordon. He'd flung himself back into the armchair again. He was useless.

Dad read the notice board for tenants while Annie dialled the number. He had his back to her and his hands in his pockets. Tina answered the phone with her usual cheery hello.

'Hi babes,' she said when she realised it was Annie. 'Having a lovely time? I'm so jealous – a weekend in the city. We're missing you.'

Annie asked for Mum but Tina told her she was out. She didn't know when she'd be back; she'd slipped out without Tina knowing.

'The house is so quiet,' said Tina, 'hurry home babes.'

'Everything alright?' asked Dad when Annie put the phone down.

'She wasn't in,' said Annie.

Mum hadn't told him about the lodgers. It was none of his business, she said. Annie couldn't tell Dad about them, in case he let on he knew to Mum and then Mum would be cross with Annie. And anyway, how could she tell him about all the new people? The ones Annie had got to know since Dad had left.

Dad put his hands up.

'Nothing to do with me anymore,' he said, like he thought Annie was lying, that Mum was in really.

106

'You don't have to tell me anything,' he said, 'I won't interfere.'

That meant the lodgers were her other life. Mum and the lodgers, they were one life and this was the other.

Annie went to bed before Dad. The duvet was thick and heavy and the sheet felt rough. Dad didn't do ironing.

The streetlight outside the bedroom window was on and its orange light glowed behind the curtains. Annie hadn't noticed the curtains when they were open, only that they were long and had some sort of old-fashioned leaf pattern. Now, with the orange light behind, she could see the faces. Old men with wild hair and open mouths, the hair shooting upwards, the gaping mouths calling out. She couldn't hear what they were saying, it was like they were behind glass, trying to make themselves heard.

Annie still wasn't asleep when Dad crept in. She could hear him taking his clothes off, the rattle of change in his pocket as he dropped his trousers onto the floor. She hadn't seen his pyjamas left out. She tried to listen for sounds of them going on but it was hard to tell the difference between the sounds of clothes coming off and going on. She pretended to be asleep on the edge of the bed so he would have enough room. He would be used to having the bed to himself now. A double bed, all to himself. Like Mum was used to having her double bed to herself. It was over a year now, since they had slept in that bed together. Mum even said she liked the space, she could stretch out. Annie hoped Dad didn't want to stretch out, she didn't want his toes touching her leg accidentally in the night. It was a bigger bed than Mum's, Mum hadn't got a new bed when Dad left.

Annie thought about Mum sleeping. It was hard to imagine, when she'd been so angry; you couldn't sleep if you were that angry. Maybe Mum was sitting up in bed, smoking. If, eventually, she got so tired she had to sleep, would she wake up angry? She'd have her first cigarette of the day in bed and that would remind her, of how angry she'd been during the last cigarette, the night before. About how angry she was with them, Annie and Gordon, especially Annie because she'd walked away and left her. She'd closed the door behind her without it making a sound, just a small click, as if she could get away with it, leaving her, by doing it quietly. They would be back that afternoon and she'd be waiting for them, Annie and Gordon, especially Annie and she'd finish off what she'd been saying. No one would close the door on her, walk away without expecting to hear the end of it. Her words would be ready. She might even say them quietly. If Annie wanted to shut the door quietly she could give her quiet.

How it was being left alone, in the quiet house, everyone having walked out. Even the lodger had gone out, the quietness had driven her out. She, their mother, had been left waiting all weekend, like that's all she was good for, waiting, smoking herself to death, waiting for them to come back. Dad was snoring on the other side of her and the faces in the curtains were all trying to have their say.

When Annie woke up, she was still lying on her left side, facing the curtains. She'd been wanting to turn over all night. Dad was in the kitchen; she could hear him doing the washing up from the night before. She got dressed quickly and looked around the room. Besides the bed, there was a chest of drawers and a wardrobe. Annie didn't know where Dad could have got them from. There was nothing from home. Mum hadn't given Dad any furniture. Besides the green velvet armchair. Or else Dad hadn't wanted any. That's what Mum said; that he didn't want to be reminded of his old life, of her. Dad had had on a blue and white striped night shirt; that was new. He used to wear pyjamas. His shoes looked the same, though it was hard to tell, she'd never looked at his shoes properly before. On top of the chest of drawers was a bottle of aftershave. Annie sniffed it; it didn't smell like Dad. She'd never seen aftershave in the bathroom at home. There were photos too. A school one of Annie and Gordon together – they had been forced to sit right next to each other for it. Gordon had to put his arm round Annie. He'd squeezed really hard to make sure she knew he didn't mean it. Both of them were smiling.

The second photo was of the two of them with Dad. They were on Disley Hill. It was a bit blurry. Mum had taken it. She wasn't very good at photos. Dad usually carried the camera. Mum hated him taking photos. She always had to say something. Like how he was always too busy recording life to live it. How had Dad got her to take this photo? Maybe he'd promised her it would be the last one. Annie picked up the photo to see if, close up, she could tell if any one was smiling. Their faces were too far away. Mum had stood too far away when she was taking the photo.

In the kitchen Dad had the cereal boxes lined up on the table. There was Weetabix, Shredded Wheat and Frosties. They were for Gordon, the Frosties; even though they were a baby's cereal, he still ate them. That was all he would eat. The Weetabix was for Annie, she knew. Dad didn't know she'd moved on. She and Mum both ate Special K now. She would have to get used to Weetabix again, that would be what she had at Dad's flat.

Gordon and Dad weren't talking. They were waiting for her. Gordon pushed the box of Weetabix towards her.

'These are for you,' he said. He knew she had Special K for breakfast. He was waiting to see if she'd say anything.

'Do you like Weetabix, Annie?' he asked.

Annie tried to get him to shut up by ignoring him, by getting on with taking two Weetabix out of the packet. She was trying to do it carefully. She hated the crumbs. That was why she'd changed to Special K in the first place, because of the way they fell apart.

'Annie doesn't eat Weetabix anymore,' he said to Dad.

Dad was at the sink making up glasses of Ribena for them both. He was making an effort, Annie could tell, to make things right for them. Gordon wanted to spoil it. He wanted Annie to spoil it.

'You should have said,' Dad brought the glasses to the table, 'what would you like instead? I can get it next time.'

'She has Special K,' said Gordon, 'like Mum.'

Annie had known, before he'd even said it, that he'd bring Mum into it.

Dad put Shredded Wheat into his bowl as if nothing had happened, as if they should carry on with breakfast as normal.

'Well isn't this nice,' he said looking from Gordon to Annie and back again, 'my family together.'

They left too early and got back to Ashbury twenty minutes before Mum was expecting them. Dad said they'd have to wait, he didn't want Mum accusing him of something.

'This is stupid,' said Gordon, 'I'm fed up with it.' But he didn't get out of the car.

'Don't blame me,' said Dad. And Gordon didn't. Neither did Annie. They knew Mum was at home waiting.

Dad wanted to get out of the car to stretch his legs. They all got out. Annie went to look in the shop windows. There was a display of gloves and hats and scarves, on faceless dummies. Gordon leant against the car and Dad walked slowly up and down the same bit of pavement, swinging his legs forward, making his stride long.

When it was time, Dad took them round the corner. They could see the house from there. Annie tried to see if there was anyone standing at the bay window, but they were still too far away. At least Mum wouldn't have spotted Dad. He gave Annie her bag.

'Will you manage?' he asked, 'it's not far.'

He pulled them both into him.

'You know I can't come with you, don't you?'

Annie's face was pressed against his jacket, so she didn't have to answer.

She knew he was watching them as they walked down the street. When they got to the front door she waved back at him, a signal that he could go; he'd have to be gone before they could ring the doorbell.

Annie wanted to stand behind Gordon, but he wouldn't let her. He was going to be the one to ring the door bell so she had to stand by the door knob, the place where Mum would appear, still angry, when she opened the door. Gordon pressed the bell. He let it ring for too long. It sounded impatient.

Mum was there before it had even finished. She was in her normal clothes, her home clothes and her slippers. She was smiling and holding out her arms to them both. Gordon let her put her arm round his neck and pull the top of his head down to kiss his hair. He got past her and into the house. That left Annie and Mum put both her arms round her.

'Hello love,' she said and her voice was quiet. Quiet like at bedtime, when the day was over.

Annie put her arms round Mum's waist. She couldn't tell where Mum was looking; if she was looking up the road after Dad. But then she felt Mum holding her face; she was looking at her. She looked in Annie's face, with her thumb on Annie's cheeks as if she was looking for tears to wipe away.

'You're home now,' she said, pulling the door shut behind them, 'back with me.'

NICHOLAS HOGG

Happy Birthday

Today is my birthday. I point the pistol I've been given as a present from the van window. I laugh and point at the head of a man who's pulled up at the lights next to me. He thinks I'm going to kill him. He doesn't see the plastic Sheriff's badge on my luminous vest, or the plastic handcuffs I've hooked on the belt loop of my orange work trousers. He screeches through the red light, swerving traffic onto the hard shoulder.

I laugh, guiltily, turning twenty-four in a beaten up transit van.

Sunrise to sunset I resurface roads across the East Midlands, carrying pots of boiling tar, glueing hands and scorching flesh. Some days it feels like purgatory, waking up before dawn or not sleeping at all. I hop over bubbling pools with men who could be a gang of grim reapers, their crooked shadows formed from clouds of steam, shovels raised above heads.

My workmates and I, the drunks and addicts, thugs and thieves.

But then a lunch break, and I'll find myself on the edge of a field eating sandwiches I made in the dark that morning, the sun-blessed corn in motion, the gang quiet and still, drinking tea from flasks or doing crosswords. These misfits, these terse and occasionally violent men, standing over a stream and naming the fish.

I like to write about these things. Secretly. I have a little notebook that fits in my back pocket. If any of the others knew I wrote they'd think me odder than they already do, a man with a degree shovelling stone.

I told Jez not to tell anyone I had a psychology bachelor, but he confided in Greebo, who confided in everyone. Now my nickname is *Psycho*. The more paranoid on the gang believe I'll read their mind, discover what depraved thoughts linger in their subconscious, and have them arrested Or worse, committed.

Jez got me the job. He cut 'Jez' into his arm with a broken bottle two years ago. You can read his name by the scars if you forget. He has that wired leanness between a junkie and long-distance runner, a skinny kid with a drug habit and guitar.

He chants, 'Greebo, Greebo, Greebo,' as he rolls another joint, skilfully crumbling tobacco as Greebo swings us through a roundabout.

Greebo has a steel plate in his skull. He failed to ride a motorbike through a patio door at a party, 'Yonks ago.' That was in the heyday of 70s bike gangs, bearded drunks in pub car parks swinging chains like warring Vikings. Now his hair is grey and tattoos faded, his head hurts in the cold.

He drives us back to the country lane we sprayed and stoned this afternoon, a tour of the flatlands and industrial estates of the East Midlands, the dead canals and flooded quarries, pit towns that time forgot when the coal ran out.

White dust, thrown up from the traffic, hovers in the indigo sky. I hang off the side door, lift up the orange cones and throw them to Jez who stacks. When we see the pavement swept and loose stone rolled, there's satisfaction, a job well done.

'Right,' announces Greebo, steering with one hand and knocking back a can of Tennants with the other. 'Time to get gone.'

Until Monday morning we've finished resurfacing. Jez leans over to Greebo, that near the wheel he could drive himself. Greebo shouts, 'What are you playin' at?' as Jez starts singing, a worthy impression of Robert Smith from The Cure. *'Tuesday, Wednesday heart attack, Thursday I don't care about that.'* Greebo tells him to 'Gerrout out of it,' but Jez tugs on his beard and finishes the line, *'It's Friday I'm in love.'*

The van veers over the white line as Greebo fights off Jez. 'You need a pint, quick. That wacky baccy's sent you nuts.'

We're going to The Grove, a snooker club and bar. The rest of the gang will be there, the tipper drivers and line painters, the angry foreman with a smile on his face, all drunk in their work clothes.

And what you think you can smell the moment you open the rattling door and pass through to fags and beer, frying chips and stale ashtrays, is failure. You're wrong. This is freedom. A retreat from gas bills and council tax, the leaky sink that needs repairing, the bastard boss and a nagging wife, a football team fighting relegation.

Not failure, but a refuge from it. And a place where miracles occur, where men on incapacity benefit lean over snooker tables and cannon balls into corner pockets. A bar you can walk out richer than when you walked in. Or poorer. Or in debt. A week's wage won and lost on the deal of a card, that ball in the corner.

This is where I skipped class, messed up my A-levels. Instead of trigonometry from textbooks I learnt about angles with a pool cue. But this was before university, before I was a real student. *Student*, a dirty word here. A word that translates into 'traitor' in a roomful of men who've worked all their lives.

A place where an education does have value is on the quiz machine. Players call me over for a cut of their winnings. I know things like who wrote *The Seagull*, the founders of Cubism, in what book Holden Caulfield is the protagonist. A week ago I stood at the end of a job with a Stop-Go board in one hand, and *The Catcher in the Rye* in the other. I let the traffic pass every two pages.

But tonight we're here to make merry, to get drunk and celebrate my birthday. Jez and I wear clean clothes we took to work in plastic bags, the tar and oil aftershave beneath a new shirt and jeans. Greebo washes the worst from his hands with a rag doused in diesel.

Then through that door, the bank of smoke, the music, always a ding-a-ling hit from the 1960s, time travel to the good old days – if you believe the barflies. Back to the golden age of a night out on a pound, ten pints and a bag of chips, and still change in your pocket for the bus fare home.

But *this is now*. We see Richie Reynolds lining up balls on the pool table. By day Richie works on the tar truck. At night he steals cars. One, maybe two a night. Add this up over a few years, and you have thousands. And *never* caught. For the moment he entertains himself setting up trick shots, a ball in every pocket and the white left spinning.

When he lifts his face from the cue, the first thing you see is the missing half of his left ear, grazed off when he rolled a convertible. Then the rude scars of unstitched cuts, the broken nose and missing eyebrow. But most striking of all is the impish grin of a cheeky boy trapped in a hooligan's body. And with this grin, the glitter behind the mask of a thief, come the women who think they have him tamed. From fishwives of the estates to the kept women bored with rich husbands.

'This one I call the birthday boy.'

Richie chips the white off the table. I catch it before it hits the floor. All this is too much for Greebo, too fast for an old man.

'Enough of playing silly buggers with you lot.'

'Got your arrows?' asks Richie.

Greebo taps his top pocket. 'I'd give you game if you were good enough.' He'll be at the dartboard all night, lost in thud and subtraction, pints of mild.

We sit and Jez buys the first round of drinks. Richie looks across the room, no women but the dolled-up with their husbands, a Friday night treat of public accompaniment.

Jez returns with three pints and a whisky, 'For the birthday boy.' We clink glasses and toast. I take a sip then set the beer down on the table.

'Drink up,' snaps Richie. 'This place is a morgue.'

We walk from The Grove, past the mobile burger van, over a crossroads with a pub on each corner, past the church and the Chinese takeaway, and into the poorly-lit Conservative Club car park. Richie asks if I want to see a skeleton key and pulls a screwdriver from his pocket. Jez giggles, drunk and stoned. We walk the rows of cars until Richie suddenly stops.

'Did someone call a taxi?'

'Into town, boss.'

'And your bird?'

Jez laughs. Richie stabs in the screwdriver up to the hilt, twisting and turning until the buckled lock breaks.

'Bingo.'

He jumps in and flicks open the passenger door. Jez lifts the handle. 'What you hanging around for?'

I'm about to run the other way when two men walk from the club.

'Get in.'

And I do.

Richie rips off the plastic ignition cover. He tears at it like a child unwrapping a Christmas present. Then the wires, tugging out a handful from the steering column. He chooses two, touches the exposed copper and sparks up the engine.

'We have *lift off!*' shouts Jez.

Richie holds himself between the seats and looks directly through the back window. He reverses from the car park. The two men in shirts and ties run down the steps, shouting, calling out like good relatives with something we left behind.

From the entrance Richie whips the steering wheel, jams the clutch, and shifts into first. Wrong way up a one-way street, an oncoming car flashes and sounds the horn. Richie rocks up the kerb, drops gears and churns lawns, flaring mud and grass as we cut across a garden before bouncing onto the carriageway, screeching out a U-turn that spans all four lanes. I slide across the back seat and stick to the door. When Richie straightens to pull away, the tail end flicks out. He rights it hard and forces the car on.

'*Still smokin'*,' whoops Jez.

The wheels are spinning in third gear as Richie accelerates, weaving from lane to lane.

'Mirror Jez.'

'Ay?'

'Turn it in,' says Richie. 'I don't want it.'

Jez flicks down the window and flattens the mirror against the car. Richie slams up the rear view mirror, reaches out and smashes off the wing mirror. It hits the road and explodes into glitter. He engine brakes onto a roundabout and spears the circle, directly passing cars on the inside lane to cut them off at the exit in a fanfare of horns.

I ask about the mirrors, shouting over the thrashed engine.

'What's in front what counts,' he answers. 'Why look back when you're goin' forwards?'

'What about a chase?'

'Every time I look to see how close they are, I'm losin' road. You're a blind man drivin' if you're not lookin''.

Street lamps brighten the dual carriageway, emphasising the black beyond the city, like a bridge of light suspending us over the dark.

Close to a hundred Richie adjusts his seat flat and tells me to take the wheel. He centres the car over the cat's eyes and slips into the back, leaving us driverless and drifting towards the central reservation. I climb past and take the steering wheel, nervous, gripping too hard.

'Imagine you're holdin' an egg,' instructs Richie.

'An egg?'

'A huge egg. If you grip the egg too hard you're gonna crush it, too soft and you'll drop it.'

I ease my grip, think of the precious egg, and stamp on the accelerator. I feel the floor of the car beneath the pedal. I can hear Jez shouting, no, singing, the tune and lyrics lost in the roar of flaming petrol and furious pistons, the tamed explosion at the end of my toes. I feel the whole thing could come apart in my hands, just the three of us jetting the blurred road, flying. No need for a car at the speed of light.

'Roundabout,' shouts Jez. He's frantically pointing, afraid I haven't seen the island. Richie tells me not to turn off. I change down gears heel toe, and power into the middle lane. I circle the island. Jez leans against the door as the car tilts and squeals.

'*Now*,' Richie shouts. 'Next exit.'

I glance over my shoulder to a blaze of headlights. I hesitate, and then swerve from the roundabout, missing a van by inches. The traffic, the van and cars, slide to a standstill. All sound their horns.

'No way,' exclaims Jez. 'How close was that?'

'Decisions,' says Richie. 'No messing about asking yourself yes or no.'

Now the road is unlit, hedges and kamikaze moths stream the headlights.

'Boom,' says Richie. 'Life. You do it then you're dead.'

The beaten engine smells like burning rubber. Parked on the edge of town, behind a knitwear factory with broken windows, another abandoned warehouse, and a nightclub, we watch the stragglers leaving, kicked out or carried out, the drunks fallen asleep in the toilet, men with sick on their shirts. And the girls who've waited for a doorman to take them home, smoking, cold in cheap dresses on a late summer night. No clouds to hold the heat, but no stars either, blazed away by the amber street lights.

This time I smoke and convince myself it'll clear my head. And not a cigarette. I hold my breath, exhale, feel the weight of a spinning earth loosen from my limbs. Richie takes back the spliff, inhales, then blows perfect smoke rings through the open window. 'How's your birthday so far?'

I tell him the time, that it's over.

'You ain't a year older till the sun comes up.'

'Anyway,' says Jez. 'You ain't had your present yet.'

'I can't wait.'

Richie smiles. 'You can write about it in your little book.'

'What?'

I pretend to know nothing about 'a little book', but Richie never misses a trick. Nothing. I've been with him in the van on a motorway, followed his pointed hand to a speck on a blue sky, a kestrel, a red kite. For a man so casual with violence, a man who once kidnapped his ex-girlfriend's new boyfriend and tortured him in a rented garage, he's capable of such tender kindness. A week ago he scooped up a handful of orphaned ducklings from a hard shoulder, cheeping over a run-down mess of feathers. He wrapped them in his jacket, took them home and set them on his little pond. He fed and kept them in a shoebox. When they were big enough to return to the wild he took them to work in the van, flapping and quacking between the shovels and cones. He stopped by the reservoir and floated each one onto the lake, the look on his face like a mother watching her first child through the school gates.

'And what about my little book?'

'You tell me.'

I feel like a border guard. Richie is a man on the threshold of my secret kingdom, awaiting permission to enter.

He asks me to read something from it. 'What's the point in writing stuff down if no one else is gonna hear it.'

I take a chance. I let him pass. Or maybe I have no choice? I pull the notebook from my back pocket and read a poem about a badger we buried last week, a job for the council called in by a passing motorist who saw the black and white body on a verge.

When I finish reading it's that quiet in the car I can hear tobacco burn in the cigarette as Richie inhales. I'm as a nervous as a convict awaiting sentence.

'That was sound.' Jez breaks the silence. 'You gave me a proper buzz. I remember that badger.'

And even this much reaction feels good. But I wait for Richie, still smoking, down to the filter as always. He flicks the cigarette butt from the window, a flurry of sparks when it strikes the ground.

'*Bearers of the dark*,' he quotes. 'I like that. How we picked him up and put him in the ground. All careful, like we were afraid of waking him up.'

Richie rests his hands on the steering wheel. He looks from the open window, checks the sky.

'You know what,' he says. 'Time to go and get your present.'

We walk across the empty car park. The last taxis have come and gone from the nightclub. The eastern sky is tinged with cyan. And quiet, just the buzz of street lights, a distant police siren wailing across town. At the back of the building, over a barbed-wire fence, we start climbing the metal fire escape. I ask where we're going, and Richie stops, turns with a finger to his lips.

First, second, third floor. We're heading for the club on the fourth. And I hope for something innocuous, like watching sunrise from the roof.

At the top, before the closed door, Richie stops, looks across town, the empty streets and derelict factories. Rows of slated roofs. He puts his hands on the rail like a preacher at a pulpit. I wait with Jez on the steps below, cold, shivering a little. Richie looks down, past Jez. I'm frightened by the force of his stare, his measured thought.

'Listen,' he says. 'After you get this *present*, I don't want you turning up for work on Monday morning.' He spits over the rail. 'Get it?' I nod, though not sure why until he adds, 'What are the the rest of us supposed to dream about if you're shovelling stone?'

Then he takes a step back from the exit. 'Happy Birthday.' He lifts his right leg and kicks, splintering the door open.

The club is deserted, an empty dance floor. No flashing lights or glitter ball twirl. Richie and Jez storm in. I follow, the reluctant robber.

Or am I? All I have to do is walk away. But the rush of breaking in prickles my skin. And the fact this is being done for me, my birthday.

Richie walks between the tables and chairs toward the bar, the register.

'How do you know they ain't cashed up?' asks Jez.

Richie laughs. 'Because I robbed the manager last month. Getting into his car with five grand.' He hops the counter, looks at the till for about a second, then hauls it onto the floor. He scans the room, the closed entrance. 'Pass that extinguisher.' I heft the red cylinder over the counter. Richie grips the handle, takes a deep breath and lifts it shoulder high. And down. Deft with shovel or pick, he sets about smashing open the cash drawer as though digging up a strip of road.

Jez stands on the counter, reading whisky labels. He snatches down a single malt, twists off the optic and swigs, screwing up his face. 'Have a go on that.' I catch the thrown bottle and drink.

Richie is committed to finishing a job he's started. The metal ring of extinguisher on register gets louder and louder, the buckled drawer coming apart with each blow.

Jez swigs from bottles of port and sherry, a magnum of champagne showered after popping the cork into the ceiling.

But then a real *bang*.

And this pop's louder than a stopped cork.

Plaster showers from the ceiling. Jez dives off the bar like a goal keeper saving a penalty in a cup final.

I hit the floor. But before another shot caroms through the room, I do what the voice commands, '*Get up!*'

When I turn and stand, hands to the roof, I see that Jez and Richie reach up, too. Palms high before a fat man in a dressing gown with a smoking gun. One of those gleaming shotguns you see nestled in the crook of men's arms with pheasants dangled over their shoulders. He sweeps both barrels from the end of the bar to Richie, takes a step closer. 'I know your face.' He prods the barrels into his chest. 'You cheeky sod. Twice in a month.'

Richie doesn't blink. 'You got one cartridge. You gonna shoot us all with a magic bullet?'

The bald man laughs, a snigger. 'No. But once your chest is gone I don't reckon your mates'll be up to much.' He quickly looks us over. 'I dump the weight of them two before breakfast.'

Then he thumbs back the hammer. Jez shakes, wets himself, a dark stain down the insides of his jeans. And for the first time since I've known Richie, I see him afraid.

But this man doesn't know it's my birthday. That I'm twenty-four and carry a toy gun. And he doesn't know it won't put a hole in his skull when I level it at his bald head and walk, commanding he lower a metal shotgun with my plastic pistol.

I surprise myself, the way I walk with the toy as if I might really kill. The way I order him to his knees.

We take the money and leave him on the floor, a dressing-gowned monk in prayer, his shotgun broken in two over the counter.

And so suddenly we're running down the steps of the fire escape, falling into each other on the metal landings, tumbling into the car.

Before Richie spins us from the car park, the man I held captive with a water pistol throws the extinguisher at us from the top floor. Richie swerves. It rings like a church bell when it hits the tarmac.

Richie screeches red lights and junctions, the dead ends and one-way streets, till we're clear of the city and heading into the glow of a coming dawn. Jez pulls bills from beneath his shirt and throws them into my lap. Thousands of pounds. I say we should share it.

'Don't be so ungrateful,' snaps Richie.

'It's the thought that counts,' laughs Jez, still trembling, passing Richie the single malt he ran with from club. Richie tips the bottle and gulps before handing it to me. I drink and feel the burn to my stomach.

'Where are we actually getting away to?' I ask, the breeze from the open window fluttering money across the backseat.

Richie turns, smiling. 'To pay our respects.'

Again we drive through the old pit towns, the patchwork fields of corn and cows, pig farms and reservoirs, acres of redbrick estates. Then past the council depot, the heaps of stone and grit where yellow trucks stand like ranks of troops.

'Take a good look at them gates,' says Richie. 'Because you ain't going through 'em again.'

And now he heads to the lane where we buried the badger, to the black-and-white flash of fur we'd silently lowered into the earth, the wooden crucifix I tied with string and fixed in the verge.

119

Mist hovers, grass sparkles with dew. In the hedgerows spider webs glint with dawn. Richie slows, winds down the window and pours a little whisky onto the grave.

But he doesn't stop.

I glance for the rear view mirror, the one he slammed away when we first got in the car, when it was still my birthday. Then Richie puts his foot down and fires us into the rising sun. That fast you'd think him afraid of the darkness chasing behind.

JOSHUA LOBB

I Forgot My Programme So I Went To Get It Back or 101 Reasons

R easons not to say anything:

1.   You don't want to make a fuss.
2.   You don't want to make this any more complicated than it is.
3.   He won't remember anyway.
4.   It's nice enough that the usher said she'd get the House Manager. This is London, after all.
5.   You don't want to have to buy another one. £3.50. Think of the exchange rate.
6.   She didn't need to bother. The theatre was all locked and they were just about to go home. She could have said No or You'll have to buy a new one or You came all the way back up that long street for a stupid programme?
7.   She could have stood there in that stolid stony-faced English way and frozen you out. Instead she said Oh let me see if – just wait there. And fetched the House Manager.
8.   You're standing there, sweaty from the sudden turn around and the rush back up the black-lit London street. Your Fortnum and Mason's carry bag filled to the brim with tourist-detritus: postcards from the National Portrait Gallery and a re-filled water bottle and an umbrella and a half-eaten Double Decker bar.
9.   Nobody likes sweat.
10. She went that extra mile for you. And now the House Manager's gone that extra mile for you. The least you can do is thank him politely and get out of there.
11. It's late.
12. The moment has passed to say anything.
13. You should have said it as soon as he came through the auditorium doors. What a thing to remember.

14. Let's face it: you don't have any proof that you bought one in the first place. And he's just unlocked the cupboard with all the programmes – all the £3.50 programmes – and he's handing it over to you.
15. He had to squat down to get to the cupboard. Cut him some slack.
16. You may have to get into a conversation about the play. The play was not really worth talking about. Not awful – not like some plays you remember – but not worth talking about.
17. He couldn't care less what you think, I'm sure.
18. Be grateful that he's not making you pay for a new programme.
19. He's probably heard it all before.
20. And – even now with your student days behind you – £3.50 is a lot of money.
21. You're in London, not Sydney.
22. You're grown men, not students.
23. You're fat now. You've got a beard.
24. He could say It's bad enough that I had to come all this way down the stairs through the auditorium doors down the access ramp and squat down in front of the programmes cupboard: now I have to engage in an awkward conversation?
25. What would you say, anyway?
26. The Fortnum and Mason's bag is heavy. You still have to lug it all the way back down that long street.
27. There's grey in your beard. You're fat.
28. Just take the damn programme.
29. He's handing you the programme. He's being friendly. Don't make this awkward.
30. There's awkward, and there's awkward. Don't go there.
31. Yes, you did say something when he came through the doors, but he may not have heard it.
32. He's busy. He's had a long night.
33. You said Oh I know you, and he didn't respond. Just leave it at that.
34. Oh I know you is not something that you want to hear when you're busy, when you've had a long night.
35. But he's had ample opportunity to notice me. He should recognise me.
36. It could be worse. Rather than handing me the programme, smiling politely, he could in fact have said Well! You claim to have left your programme in the auditorium but my ushers found no programme left behind. He could say My ushers have better things to do than to listen to the ravings of some fat grey-flecked beardie weirdie with a tatty

Fortnum and Mason's bag. Take your Double Decker bar and get out of here.

37. It's unlikely that he would use the phrase My ushers, not from what I remember of him.
38. It's likely to rain. You still have to traipse back down that long street carrying your packed Fortnum and Mason's bag.
39. He could have recognised you and is choosing to ignore you.
40. More probably, he doesn't recognise you.
41. It was – jesus – 15 years ago?
42. It was in Sydney, not London.
43. We were students, not grown men.
44. He probably doesn't even remember. Why should he? It wasn't his moment. It was mine.
45. It's not like it was anything memorable. One song.
46. I don't even remember his name.
47. You can't say Oh I remember you but I don't remember your name.
48. Keep it clean and simple. Let him give you the programme and get out of there.
49. Blazey's boyfriend is all I have to say.
50. I wonder if Blazey remembers?
51. I can't say You were Blazey's boyfriend, weren't you?
52. Maybe he doesn't want to remember Blazey. What if the break-up was terrible? What if he spent 15 years blotting Blazey out of his mind and now I come in with Oh I know you – you're Blazey's ex, aren't you?
53. It's stupid to say Oh I know you when you don't even remember his name.
54. And it's clear he doesn't remember me.
55. This is probably the least important moment of the day. The National Portrait Gallery and St Paul's the Actor's Church and a walk up to Islington and a night at the theatre. Don't dwell on moments.
56. He's giving you the programme. Just take the programme, you idiot.
57. What do you want to say anyway? Thank you? Thank you for what?
58. If it was important then he'd remember it.
59. It doesn't matter to him.
60. There's only so long he can squat there, his arm outstretched, offering you the programme.
61. It wasn't sexual if that's what you're thinking. Maybe he does remember and he's thinking that I was in love with him or something. It wasn't that.

62. It's too late. The moment has passed.
63. Let it go. You've got the programme in your hand now. You don't have to fork out another £3.50.
64. It was such a small moment anyway. You idiot.
65. You're an idiot. 15 years have passed and you still remember that tiny moment. Other people have let it drift away like the small moment that it was. Just one song in the night. Just one quiet moment after a horrible year.
66. It was an indulgent moment. Let it go, you idiot. One song can't save a life. One Blazey-boyfriend listening to one beardless student singing one song does not save a life.
67. It's not that I remembered it before tonight. I only remembered it when he came swinging through the auditorium doors. I'd completely forgotten about it. But it was an important moment for me.
68. He may not even remember Blazey. He may have moved to London, become a grown man, forgotten Sydney, forgotten Blazey. He may not have to hold little moments in his head. He may not need little moments to keep him moving forward, away from Sydney, from student life, from Blazey.
69. How would you even remind him? Oh I know you is all you've come up with so far and that didn't really make an impact. Probably because you don't know him. He was just Blazey's boyfriend who happened to be in the right place at the right time.
70. It may not even have mattered who had been there. It could have been any one of Blazey's boyfriends who needed to be there. Or anyone's boyfriend. Or anyone at all. The important thing is that it had to be someone who I didn't know. Someone outside the horribleness of that year.
71. How can you remind someone who you don't know of a moment that will never be important to them?
72. The usher's locked up. They all want to go home.
73. 4 o'clock in the morning after the cast party for that awful student play that Blazey and I were in and me wanting to kill myself.
74. A darkened bedroom in the cast-party house. The noise of the rest of the cast ripping through from the lounge room.
75. Me getting up to go home and thinking I'm going to go home and kill myself.
76. Me having planned to kill myself throughout that whole horrible year.
77. Me mentally running the bath and laying out the pills and wanting so much to have that horrible year over and done with.

78. I was a student after all. Melodrama comes easily.

79. We'd escaped from the ripping-air cast party of an awful play. The world's stupidest director and the world's most irritating lead actor and the world's most embarrassing stage fighting you have ever seen.

80. I've never been satisfied with theatre. If he was to say to me tonight Here's your programme, I hope you enjoyed your night, I'd end up saying The staging was great but I didn't like the representation of women.

81. It's statements like that which make people say That'll be £3.50, thank you.

82. We were sitting in the dark and Blazey was singing songs from *The Muppet Show* and I was talking about Gonzo's great song from *The Muppet Movie*.

83. And not just the awful play. My father being an arsehole and my mother being dead and 1994 being the world's most horrible year and that fight with Amy and not knowing where that anger came from. The air ripping that whole year.

84. What a great song. Better than the ordinary play tonight and the awful play 15 years ago. Better than dead mothers and heavy Fortnum and Mason's bags. Better than polite awkward exchanges between the House Manager of the Almeida Theatre and a tourist from Australia.

85. And the room was still and quiet and the air did not rip. And Blazey singing Miss Piggy singing *What Now, My Love?*

86. Me going on and on about Gonzo's song from *The Muppet Movie*.

87. And me almost not wanting to kill myself.

88. Me half-up off the floor and him – Blazey's boyfriend, who I never knew before that night and never saw again – saying Don't go, sing that song you like.

89. Him saying Here's a replacement programme. And then going back through the swinging doors into the auditorium.

90. It's silly. Maybe it was Blazey who said Don't go, sing that song. Maybe he couldn't even care less about Gonzo's song. Maybe he was thinking Dear God, you idiot, I'm with Blazey, get out of this darkened room and leave us alone. But that's not how I remember it.

91. The cast party and my arsehole father almost not mattering any more.

92. The ordinary play and the heavy bag and the almost-rain not figuring at all.

93. I'd be happy to pay the £3.50. I can claim it on tax if you give me a receipt.

94. You choosing to ignore the Oh I know you. Or perhaps not hearing it at all. Perhaps not seeing the flash of recognition in my face or perhaps thinking God it's late, can't I please just go home?

95. Of course I remembered that moment before I saw you again tonight. I remember it often. You let me sing that song in the dark and because of that I didn't go home and kill myself. Yes, I probably wasn't actually going to kill myself – I was a student after all – but you stopped me anyway. You said Don't go, sing that song you like. Blazey lay on the bed in the darkened bedroom, her head (I think) in your lap and you let me sing.

96. Gonzo's song from *The Muppet Movie:*
there's not a word yet for old friends who've just met
part heaven, part space – or have I found my place?
you can just visit, but I plan to stay
I'm going to go back there some day
I'm going to go back there some day.

97. And it made me feel better. And I didn't go home and kill myself.

98. The usher's gone home.

99. And when I do want to kill myself I remember that moment: 4 o'clock in the morning during the worst, most horrible year of my life in the dark singing Gonzo's song for Blazey and Blazey's boyfriend who I never saw again until tonight. That moment has saved me many times and I want to thank you for that. I'm sorry it's late and you had to come down through the swinging doors and unlock the programme cupboard and squat down and get out another programme for a now-fat beardie weirdie but I thank you. I wish it were possible for me to thank you.

100. You left the theatre half an hour ago. You're now on the street, further down from where you turned, suddenly, after rootling through your silly Fortnum and Mason's carry bag, shoved with your water bottle and your umbrella and a nostalgically half-eaten Double Decker bar and a book and some liquorice all-sorts and a stash of postcards from the National Portrait Gallery, and noticed that you must have left your programme behind. But that was ages ago now. 15 years and an infinitely-paused moment of a grown man giving another grown man a programme to replace the one he left in the auditorium. Keep walking and put all that behind you.

Reasons to say something:
1. You saved my life once. And I thank you for that.

ANNEMARIE NEARY

Siren

Belfast was tight and hard and grey. No wonder, for it scowled under Cave Hill and caught its rain and most days black billows replaced the sky. For all the grey, colour screamed out from tattered flags and from the yellow shipyard cranes. As for the "situation", as they called it on the news, it was bad. However bad it got, though, her Ma always had the same thing to say.

'There'll be worse to come yet.'

And there was. Much worse.

Even her name was a diminutive. Roisin, little rose. A flower of a thing, a wee dote. Rowsheen. She was eager and dutiful and dull.

Dolores, though, was different. In class, she sat in disdainful absence, her face all sharps and flats. She wore an Afghan coat over her school uniform and earrings that swung as far as her chin. There were whispers of a married man somewhere up the Antrim Road.

'Are you on for a bit of craic?'

Dolores had never seemed to notice her before. It came out of the blue, in the dinner queue, over the cake and custard. Normally, Dolores hung out with a mousey wee one from the Markets who acted as her skivvy. She didn't bother much with anyone else. She'd come from Craigavon after mid-term break. Burned out of the house, people said. Da on the run, they said. Involved? Mebbe.

'Somewhere new, where you don't get the same saddos every week?' She looked over Roisin's shoulder, chewing luxuriously, seeming not to care what the answer was. 'Well, are you into dancin' and that?' she said, then, as though Roisin was thick as pigshit.

'Aye, I suppose.'

'Friday coming then.'

Roisin hesitated. 'Is there a big crowd going?'

Dolores wrinkled her nose. 'Say nothing or they'll all want to come.'

127

And so Roisin felt chosen, as indeed she had been.

Friday evening, she waited where she'd been told, on the corner of Rebecca Street where Markey's bar used to be. The corrugated iron only went half way up so you could still see inside. The charred beams looked like black velvet. Her back pressed against the barriers, she watched the rain hover in the streetlight, putter into pavement cracks. A trickle ran down her fringe and onto her nose. She skimmed a finger under her eyes to save her mascara and waited.

Rebecca Street died when the last school kids carried their wrapped singles from the chipper. Ever since Markey's went up, the parade of shops across the way was braced with shutters and grilles. Roisin brushed a haze of raindrops off her sleeve as a clatter of hoods passed her, Docs scraping on broken glass. She wondered would Dolores turn up at all.

It was a black taxi with a dirty number-plate and a bockety door. Dolores stuck her head out the window.
    'Would you look what the cat dragged in.' Her black hair was backcombed off her forehead. 'Well, hop in, then.'
    Dolores sat up front with the driver. They talked in a mutter, like they knew each other (but maybe that's what people like Dolores did, knew people like taxi drivers, they were that used to being out and about).
    Roisin tried to make conversation, wedged herself forward on the seat. She asked Dolores what the place was like, did they play decent music? But Dolores just said it was progressive stuff and turned away. The driver's eyes flicked up at Roisin now and then. Eventually, he slid the glass hatch shut.
    They drove over to the north of the city and, before she knew it, Roisin had lost all track of where they were, the driver was making that many turns. There weren't any burnt out buses up this way, nor barricades neither. Not even that many bombsites. There were front gardens and, here and there, a swing park. It was, she thought, an odd kind of a place.

She'd lied through her back teeth to get out with Dolores. Ma thought she was with Majella Carr and Majella Carr thought she was covering up some fella. She started to worry about getting home. There's no way she was walking through Tiger Bay. She wasn't even sure she liked Dolores. She didn't really know what progressive was but it didn't sound like the Sweet.

Then, the popping of the indicator and the driver's eye in the mirror as he scanned the road behind. They stopped on a side road within sight of a plastic sign with flashing palm trees. She reached for her purse and pushed a couple of quid through the hatch but Dolores said, 'No sweat.' She smiled at her, seemed friendlier now. 'Save it for the vodkas.'

Roisin noticed the man slip Dolores something she put in her spangly bag. Maybe it was change but she didn't think so. Dolores held her bag over her head to keep off the wet and Roisin did the same even though hers was nothing worth showing off.

'By the way, I'm Dolly when I'm out.'

'What?'

'Dolly. It's got a bit more go in it. You can be Rosie, that'll do rightly.'

Roisin thought Dolly was a stupid name. She wondered if Dolores fancied herself as a go-go dancer. She didn't mind the thought of being someone else for the night, though. She'd have preferred Tanya or Natasha, some icy kind of a name would put you in mind of a Russian ballerina. Still, Rosie was easier to remember.

'I didn't realize we'd be going so far from home,' she said, 'Just for a disco. We must be nearly in Larne now.'

'Well, you're here now, aren't you,' Dolores said and played with one of her eyelashes.

Roisin glanced around to see if she could see the taxi but its lights were already disappearing around the corner onto the main road.

'Where are we anyway? There was loads of Union Jacks all the way down that road back there.'

Dolores looked irritated, started fidgeting with the other eyelash, lashes which, Roisin decided, were definitely fake.

'A wee flag's not going to hurt you. Just don't let on you've got a Taig name, that's all.' Then she laughed, but you could tell that even she knew it wasn't really funny at all.

The Copacabana Disco Club was a great big shed of a place with a thin row of Christmas tree lights over the door even though it was already March. There was a queue of girls with pinky-bluey legs and anoraks over their frocks. Nobody said much. They all just shuffled towards the man checking bags on the door. Inside, white lights whirled around the walls making mist of the smoky air. There were no palm trees. Dolores bought them both a vodka and Britvic. It smelt okay but Roisin had only had

Babycham before. It was at somebody's wedding and Ma thought it was fake stuff for the wee ones.

Dolores had a glittery top on that looked really with it. She'd drawn thick black lines under her eyes and then there were those eyelashes. Once she'd knocked back her drink, she put the spangly bag down on the floor and started to shimmy to the music, her fingers making circles in the smoky air, her body more snaky than it needed to be. She threw her head back a lot like she was laughing at something Roisin had just said. Except Roisin didn't say much. It was difficult to make conversation the music was that loud, and Roisin kind of guessed she did it for effect. Like she thought she was on a stage and everyone would be looking just at her. She was surprised Dolores liked the kind of music they were playing. She didn't think it was what you would call progressive at all.

There were an awful lot of men at the disco; grown-up kind of men. More filled out, most of them, than the fellas that hung around the chipper on Rebecca Street. Well turned out too. They lined up at the bar, peering out over the heads of their pints. The throwing the head back and the pretend laughing seemed to work because loads of men wanted to dance with Dolores. A fella would ask her to dance and, when she nodded, his mate would slip in opposite Roisin. It was like everyone was there just to worship Dolores, which didn't seem fair, really. Roisin began to get sick of this game.

'How are we getting home?'

Dolores was still jiggling around even though the fella had slunk off back to his pint. 'Brian'll be back when we're ready.'

'When's that?'

She stopped, her hands on her hips. 'Jesus, Rosie, you can be a right wee pain in the arse. Just hang on, will you. You'll get home.'

'Is Brian the taximan?'

'I can't hear a word you're saying. Taximan? Yeah, yeah. He's the taximan.'

There were lots more syrupy drinks, the men paying now. Roisin couldn't hear what anyone was saying so she just smiled, which was easy, because she felt all syrupy herself. Then a fella came and danced with Dolores and she nodded at the end of that dance and the one after that and soon they were wrapped round each other. Roisin was dancing with his mate and because she didn't want to get split up from Dolores, she kept nodding too and then she kind of leaned against him because it was easier to keep her balance that way. There was a bump in his jeans when they slow danced and he nuzzled a bit at her hair. She felt quite proud of causing the bump, even though she didn't fancy him back.

It was only when the lights went up at the end that she sneaked a proper look at him. He looked as though they hadn't got the colour mix right when it came to his skin. He was blueish with a rash of red on his chin like he might be allergic to razor blades or shaving cream or that. Otherwise, he didn't look that different from lots of other lads she knew from around the place; same skinny snipy look. Except for his lips. They were fleshy, puffed out like little pincushions. Apart from the lips, though, he had the look of someone who was always cold, like the cold kind of stuck to him.

He asked Roisin was she doing her Highers and she told him it was A Levels here but it was kind of the same. His sister was, he said. Highers, he said. Dead clever. All his vowels had the juice squeezed out of them.

'Are you Scotch, then?'

'Aye.'

His name was Ian. She didn't know too many Ians.

He took Roisin's hand and slid his bony fingers through hers. His mates were calling him and shoving their fists into the crooks of their arms. He turned his back on her and she saw him give them the fingers when he thought she wasn't looking. She wondered when this Brian one thought he was showing up. She glanced at her watch and hoped Ma had taken her tablets and wasn't waiting up for her, stewed pot on the table, worrying her head off.

He asked did she mind if he put his arm around her. She just shrugged because it seemed a bit rude to say no since he'd asked. Next thing Dolores was tapping him on the shoulder. She was all breathy and her lipstick was smudged.

'I'm just borrowing Rosie a wee tick.'

Roisin tried to ask her when Brian thought he was showing up. At first, she pretended not to hear and then she just said, 'Brian? He's deadly. God knows where he's got to. Probably drinking his head off in some club. He said he'd meet us in Glenda's anyway. Later on.'

'Glenda's? Who the hell's Glenda? Dolores?'

Dolores spun around at her and for a moment Roisin thought she might hit her. 'Dolly, you thick Arab. The name's Dolly.' Dolores spoke right into her ear and the heat from her breath felt prickly.

'We nearly done it in the car park,' she whispered.

She was all flushed and slurred but there was a glitter in her eye that was the soberest thing Roisin had ever seen. 'My one's best mates with your one. Ach, come on Rosie. You said you'd be on for the craic. Sure you're late now, anyway. You may as well be hung for a sheep as a lamb.'

She got a good look at Dolores's fella, standing over near the door with his jacket on already. He looked a bit old to be anyone's fella. He looked drunk too but maybe it was just from being with Dolores. His eyes were thirsty when he looked at her. Like he wanted to drink her in with his pint.

Ian came over and put his arm around her like he was claiming her back and it felt quite nice to be wanted since everybody else seemed to be dying for a feel of Dolores. Dolores called him love and said wouldn't he come along with Rosie to a wee bit of a party in her sister's house. Glenda, she said. Glenda was a great one for parties. Roisin didn't think Dolores had a sister at all. She thought Glenda was a Sunday school kind of a name and she wondered what kind of people call one daughter Dolores and the other one Glenda.

'Don't worry about a six pack,' Dolores said, all sweet as pie now. 'The place is coming down with booze. Just bring yourselves.'

'No,' she said. 'No mates. Just the four of us.'

Her stomach felt raw and it was freezing cold outside. They passed one street where the kerb stones were painted red, white and blue and she was afraid suddenly, and the shivering was only half from the cold. Ian began to rub her arm like it was some magic lamp, round and round in small circles like he was polishing it. After a while, he had his denim jacket whipped off him and draped it around her shoulders, which was decent of him even though it didn't make a lot of difference.

Dolores walked on ahead a bit with her fella, then she doubled back on herself like she wasn't sure which was the right street. She was looking at the street names and swearing to herself. When Dolores stopped, it was at a house a couple of streets further on.

'My head's cut with all the booze,' she said, looking pleased with herself.

'Would you look at the state you have me in,' she said to her fella and gave him a smacker right on the lips. He held onto her like his life depended on it.

The house was at the end of a row where most of the others seemed to be boarded up. Roisin began to wonder if they were in the right place at all. She wondered, too, how Dolores could get this dump of a street mixed up with the nice ones they'd been down earlier, but Dolores opened the door with a key she had in her spangly bag.

It was dead quiet in the house. There was a fire smoking in the grate and a music centre over by the far wall. One of the fellas went and had a look but there was only one record, the Bay City Rollers. Nobody admitted they wanted that on even, with them being Scotch and that, till Dolores said, sure throw it on anyway for the craic. Ian asked was there nobody else coming to the party. Dolores said they were a bit on the early side.

'Anyway, isn't it nice to have the place to ourselves for a wee while after the disco. Sure yiz wouldn't say no to a wee court, would yiz?'
    She winked at her fella and Roisin felt herself go all red. Dolores didn't seem to know where things were kept. She was opening doors, closing them again, making the kitchen echo like it was a building site and Roisin wondered how often she'd been there before and about this Glenda one, what kind she was to be living here. She wondered whether Brian was Glenda's boyfriend and what anyone could see in him. She wondered was he the married man up the Antrim Road she'd heard tell of. Dolores took some candles out of one of the kitchen cupboards and dripped the wax onto saucers before placing them in the corners of the room.

A cold white bulb hung over the sofa with a plastic shade around it, white too, shaped like petals. The sofa was stained velveteen, and there wasn't even a carpet on the floor. Roisin felt ashamed of the place, for Dolores' sake. To be taking visitors to a dump like this. She wished they could get rid of the white light burning because it was doing her head in and then, as though she'd read her mind, Dolores turned it off.

It was even worse with the light off.
    'If you hate me after what I say, blang blang,' sang the Bay City Rollers, and her head was beginning to ache after all the vodka.

There was plenty of beer. Someone had left a pile of it in the corner: Tennents and Bass and Smithwicks. Dolores was handing out cans and Ian took one in each hand and said cheers. Next thing, Dolores was knocking one back herself with her feet slung over the edge of the sofa.

Dolores told them her name was Dolly and Roisin thought that was a bit odd, nearly having it off with a fella in the carpark and not even having got that far.

'Well, hello Dolly,' her fella said.

'Yeh, yeh, yeh,' she said back and stuck out her tongue at him even though he wasn't taking the piss, just trying to get a laugh. She patted the sofa beside her and he came and sat down and next thing they were all over each other. Roisin tried not to look.

You could tell Ian was trying not to look either for he was twitching around in his seat. All of a sudden, he stood up and walked a bit around the room like he was searching for something to distract him. His feet scraped on the bare boards like there were steel tips on his boots. She wondered what he thought was on the menu next and she started to work out in her head how long it would take to walk home.

Dolores was making little moans that you could hear in the space between tracks on the album and her fella had his head buried somewhere between her boobs. There was a baldy patch at the back of his head. Roisin caught Dolores' eye even though she was trying not to and the glitter was still there as she looked out over his head. She took him upstairs then and Roisin wondered where that left her and the lift home.

It was a funny place to live. There was no sign of a life at all. No photos, no posters on the walls, no magazines, food, nothing. Just the candles and the beer and the Bay City Rollers. Underneath a helmet of slack, the fire smoked and struggled. Ian picked up a poker from beside the grate and shoved it into the centre and little yellow tongues began to dart out here and there. They sat opposite one another for a while, like Darby and Joan, him in his brown armchair and her in her brown armchair, one on either side of the fire. At least there was the fire to watch now, she thought. Then Dolores shouted down from upstairs that Glenda would be back soon with her man.

'She won't be too pleased if she finds you pair using up her fire on her. Yiz better come upstairs and I'll sort her out later on.'

Roisin didn't want to go upstairs in case it gave him ideas but he seemed to guess what she was thinking and he said not to worry. There was a strip light that hopped into life when he flicked the switch. It rained down a vinegary light, like in a chipper. The room was small with two divans and wallpaper with brown and orange flowers on it. She sat on the end of a bed because there was nowhere else. He sat on the end of the other one. They sat there a while, not saying much, her still in his jacket, till he asked did she mind if he switched the light off. She said she did, kind of, because she didn't want her bones jumped. He said not to worry about that too. It was just nicer to wait in the dark, he said. Because after all they both had to wait. Her for her lift, and him? For his mate, maybe. The place smelt gassy. Damp, maybe. Or something dead under the floorboards. Outside there was a street light which shone in. Not quite like a moon.

She was listening for Dolores in the next room. Straining to hear when they were finished so she could get home.

'I'll be killed for being out this late,' she told him.

'Aye, it's late alright.'

'So what brings you to Belfast then?'

'Just a wee bit of construction work,' he said, 'Don't mind it too much. It's not that different from home.'

'Same crap weather?'

'Same crap everything.'

She felt queasy from all the vodka and orange and cold even with the jacket on. He told her he was from Livingston and she said, I presume, and he tickled her under the arms. He asked her what she wanted to do when she left school. She said she wanted to be a nurse even though she didn't. Next door, the bed was rattling away and Dolores was yelping. He kissed her neck then, little soft kisses, and she pictured the lips like little pincushions and how it was them was making this feeling she had. She relaxed then and let him just kiss her because it was easier than trying to figure out everything.

He said she was lovely. Said something about a real Irish colleen. And she thought that was funny because that's what her Da used to call her when she was a wee one, his *cailín deas*, his *Róisín dubh*, his wee black rose with the streely hair. She thought colleen was a strange kind of a word for him to be using for you only saw it nowadays on plastic dolls or

Americans on the telly and it's not something you'd think they'd hear tell of in Livingston or wherever.

She thought she heard the door banging downstairs and she started worrying how Dolores was going to explain to Glenda about them drinking the beer and using up the fire and all being upstairs. She pulled back from him and listened for the sound of voices from down below.

But then he was kissing her and soon she was kissing him too and telling herself the sound must have come from some other house and sure anyway Glenda must be expecting them back if Brian knew to come here to pick them up. She was lying down on the bed now and their legs were getting tangled up and she could feel the bump again, where it nestled in at her thigh and she started to feel she would like to touch it and they were kissing deeper now and wider. There was a hum in her head that blocked out everything else. The kissing made her someone who wasn't in Belfast any more, some place much warmer and brighter and greener. Like she was in that shampoo ad.

Then, all at once, the light was on and the room was full of voices and metal and heavy bodies. Someone pulled her by the ankle and she hit her head on something hard as she slid off onto the floor. She kicked out and one of them yelled that she was a stupid cunt. The others were shooting by then. It was like being inside a machine and she couldn't see anything because someone had her by the hair and was flinging her against a wall on the landing, just beside the banisters. It rocked as she hit it and she thought of those houses in Coronation Street that wobble every time someone runs down the stairs.

She crouched there with her thumbs jammed in her ear drums, fingers pressed hard into her eyeballs, chin in her knees. She might have wet herself but all she could think of was the loyalists and their knives and the back of her neck all exposed and how she was a sitting duck nearly in Larne in the house of someone called Glenda. Even though she couldn't bear to see what was happening, she couldn't help opening her eyes a slit just in case she might be able to get away before they noticed her.

Through the banisters, a pair of runners, dirty white with two blue streaks on the side, then a pair of desert boots. She heard them thud down the stairs and the scrape of something metal along the wall. It was then that she saw Dolores standing with the zip undone on her skirt and no tights on and a man who might have been Brian with his tongue in her mouth. She shut her eyes tight again to get back to that lovely green field she'd been in before with the floaty music.

'Get that one the fuck out of here.'

Someone half lifted, half dragged her down the stairs and she threw up all over him and he said fuck that and she was clammy and cold and there was the sound of someone who might be her screaming. And then she just felt herself fall on concrete, that final kind of a fall when you go over the handlebars and there's nowhere further to go. Next thing, she was in the back of a car and Dolores had her face too close to hers and her lipstick was all run and her mascara made her look like a Panda and she said don't you dare boke your guts up in here and gave her a newspaper to sit on. She could smell herself now and couldn't understand how it had come to this.

'Are they dead?' she heard herself say but she didn't think anyone answered.

Ma always said there were people you just shouldn't get too close to. People who were, she said, involved. Stay well clear, she said. It's a dirty business for all the singing and the like. When you boil it all down it's just killing and the smell of killing never leaves a person. They live every day with the stink of it in their nostrils.

She started to cry, rocking herself back and forward on the back seat of the car. She didn't care they were soldiers though normally she hated soldiers like everyone else did. She didn't care about anything but poor Ian with his bad skin and his soft mouth and the way it was her fault he died because he thought she was lovely.

She could tell Dolores and the man were talking about her, could hear bits and pieces of it even though it felt they were talking on the surface and she was down with the *Titanic*. Dolores saying she'd shut her up, not to worry when he asked why the fuck she picked a spa like that.

When they got to Rebecca Street, the man opened the back door and held her tight by the shoulders. She found it hard to hold her head straight but he rapped her cheek sharply and shoved her chin up to make her look at him. That was when she realised he was worried, scared even.

'See you?' he said, and his eyes looking at every scrap of her face except her eyes, 'You done alright.'

Maybe she pulled away from him or maybe her head dropped because he slapped her again.

'One word to anyone and I'll do you.'

He let go of her then, and his voice was softer now.

'You done alright.'

Car door, engine and they were gone and there was no one there at all any more, not even her. Rebecca Street was silent but somewhere in the distance the women were out clanking at the bin lids so maybe there was a raid on in the flats.

She leant against the wall and let the rain wash her face. The street began to take shape around her; the dark husk of Markey's bar, a line of milk bottles, a Stewart's bag some wee glue-sniffer must have left behind. She noted these things in separate snap-shots. She went from one to the other, then tried them in a different sequence, but she just couldn't block out the pictures in her head. They all jangled around together, the normal things with the terrible ones. She held herself, arms crossed tight, hands pumping at the fleshy bits above her elbows until she remembered the jacket was his. She shuddered it off, then flung it as far as she could. It lay in a crumpled heap under the lamp post, gathering silvery droplets of rain while, way over to the west, the beam of a helicopter jerked across rooftops.

TERESA STENSON

In a seaside café

I look out to sea and imagine what it must have been like to really see it; not just the news footage. That wall of something that shouldn't make a wall of anything. Mum rang and I said – don't worry, it could never happen here, something to do with plates. There must have been little cafes like this one: so on-the-edge. Maybe there was an equivalent of me, waiting.

things Amy knows:
the coffee is making the old people twitch
she is the youngest manager in the whole chain
it was the sea that made her take the job
and it was the broken heart
when you reach a certain age, it matters what kind of chair you sit on
the locals don't like the refurb and they blame her a bit
nobody ever puts the newspapers back in the rack
the print on the wall is of a giant coffee bean which doesn't look like a coffee bean

I'd heard just one thing about this town before I got here, and it wasn't even a fact, just a joke someone told me once: 'There are so many old people, even the shop windows are bi-focal.' It's turned out to be a bit true. But it's out-of-season time. So I'm hoping. The important thing is that it's far away. Mum says I can go home at any time if this is not the right thing. How can I know?

In the first week a lot of conversations would go like this: "Well, of course you didn't work here before, and of course none of it is your fault. BUT. My love. Can you tell me. Why have you stopped serving scones?"

I'd say something like, "Scones are just not very Italian."

They'd say, "None of us are bleedin' Italian."

things Amy feels:
responsible for the biscotti/false teeth incident

like listening to music but it makes her think of him
annoyed at people of a certain age who assess how best to get into a
chair
like she wouldn't know what to do with a day off
that things were better when she didn't know what apathy was
sure that people look at the print of the coffee bean and think 'vagina'

He didn't even tell me with words. He just let me see the remains of their night together, two stained wine glasses by his bed. And all I could say was, 'You don't even like red wine.'

things Amy wants:
to feel like she did when she was sure of where she was from
maybe for a big wave to come and –
to never get too old to sit on something soft

There was no way to stop it; when something that big has started it's beyond saving. Displacement on a massive scale. It's internal, nothing to do with surface, the wind, or the moon. It happens inside the sea.

things Amy has:
a small flat above the café
a place at a university next year if she wants to go

There was, in the first week, a CD called 'Italian Café Songs' but the customers signed a petition to get Radio 2 on, 'like before'. Head Office said – no way. Italian Café Songs or nada. Now I hear everything – amplified conversations which aren't conversations. They filter in as I look out at the grey day and the waves. I remember how someone told me the sea could hypnotise – but then – woman with loud voice reads to husband and friends from newspaper: "GIRL, 16, ATTACKED BY GANG OF SIX MEN".
Something of a pause.
Then, "Our Kegan's the only one in our family who wears glasses, ya know."

things Amy dreams:
the world will end in five minutes

a cross between a fish and a bird and a crab is found under her bed
a woman chops off her own head with a portable guillotine

*There was no advance warning. Nothing detected. It is possible to miss
an earthquake. Just as it happened, the sea creatures, their covers ripped
off them, lay exposed on the sea bed. A whole world changed to negative.*

things Amy notices:
she's happier in the daytime
the man who delivers the milk has blue eyes
it's been a while since she heard the speech pattern of people her own
age

*"and you know Elsie, she's like me – she doesn't shut up. But that
Linda, she just sat there, face o'thunder, she*
did
not
utter
one word all night.
I says to Elsie, what's up with her? She says, well, she's depressed.
I says
why
on
earth
would that woman be depressed?
She says, well, she's 60, isn't she?
*I says, well, so am I, and look at me. I'm lovin' it. I says, I don't
understand it me, people getting depressed, there's no time in life for
that."*

things Amy hopes:
her accent hasn't changed
for the milk delivery man to say more than 'hello'
that her face hasn't gone blurry in her mother's memory

*Today the man who delivers the milk said I'm ageing prematurely. He
said I look worn and it's probably the caffeine. I told him I don't drink
coffee, and he said it must be infiltrating my body then, because I look like
it's doing me some damage. I didn't know what to say so I said nothing.*

things Amy does:
makes a sign to ask people to put their newspapers back in the rack
phones her Mum on Sundays and says everythingisokay
pulls on her cheeks when she's not okay
imagines he could walk through the door any minute to say
"I've changed my mind. I want *you*."

I took the job because of what is here and what is not. But he hasn't gone anywhere.

things Amy says:
fine, thank you
probably just watch TV

Some places by the sea build walls a few metres high to protect themselves, but what happens when the barriers aren't strong enough?
The man who delivers the milk said I look old because he was building up to asking me out. He said he knows just the thing to freshen my complexion and he winked. Like an affection-starved idiot, I laughed, and he's picking me up tomorrow at 7.

things Amy thinks:
dating is probably just what she needs
she will be funny and sexy and charming
he might want her back if he found out she was with someone else

I felt like a different girl, better and worse all at once. Pleased because I was with someone I didn't care about so maybe I'm stronger than I thought. And it was okay right up to the part where I thought about how different 'it' was to his – and then how alien, how grotesque. How easy a metre high wall can collapse.

things Amy needs:
to be on her own
to be near people

I hoped he wouldn't call and he doesn't. A different man starts delivering the milk. I feel a nip of rejection, but really this is small next to the regret that it happened at all. I wish... I wish I just knew how to –

things Amy tries:
to be okay
to stop trying to be okay

It's been so windy all weekend, then this morning so calm. All the newspapers were returned to the rack today and in the heat of the moment I switched the radio on to Radio 2. There was a small cheer, smiles of approval. There's a girl my age being transferred here to help next week. It will start to get warmer soon.

things Amy starts:
ordering scones without Head Office knowing
painting the second bedroom
listening to music

I watch the waves caused by the wind, the moon. Sweeping things away, wearing things down. Building things up.

Biographies

Jackie Kay [Poetry Judge]

Jackie Kay was born and brought up in Scotland. She has published five collections of poetry for adults – *The Adoption Papers* (winner of a Forward Prize, a Saltire Award and a Scottish Arts Council Book Award), *Other Lovers* (which won the Somerset Maugham Award) and *Off Colour* shortlisted for the 1999 TS Eliot Award, *Life Mask* and *Darling*, New and Selected Poems (both Poetry Book Society Recommendations.)

Her first novel, *Trumpet* (Picador, 1998), won the Guardian Fiction Prize, a Scottish Arts Council Book Award and The Authors' Club First Novel Award. It was also on the shortlist for the IMPAC award.

Her new collection of short stories, *Wish I Was Here,* won the Decibel Writer of the Year award. She is a fellow of The Royal Society of Literature. She is Professor of Creative Writing at Newcastle University. Her new collection of poetry for children, *Red, Cherry Red,* was published by Bloomsbury and won the CLYPE award. *The Lamplighter*, the play she wrote for the BBC to commemorate the abolition of the slave trade, has just been published. She lives in Manchester with her son.

She was awarded an MBE in 2006.

Ali Smith [Short Story Judge]

Ali Smith was born in Inverness in 1962. Her first book, *Free Love and Other Stories* (1995), won the Saltire Society Scottish First Book of the Year Award and a Scottish Arts Council Award.

Her first novel, *Like*, was published to critical acclaim in 1997. A second collection of short stories, *Other Stories and Other Stories*, was published in 1999, and *The Whole Story and Other Stories* in 2003. Her second novel, *Hotel World* (2001), won the Encore Award, a Scottish Arts Council Book Award and the inaugural Scottish Arts Council Book of the Year Award. It was also shortlisted for both the Orange Prize for Fiction and the Booker Prize for Fiction, as was her 2005 novel, *The Accidental*, which won the Whitbread Novel Award. *Girl Meets Boy* was published in 2007.

She has also published a play, *The Seer* (2006), and her most recent collection of short stories is *The First Person and Other Stories* (2008). *The Reader* (2006) is an anthology of favourite pieces of writing gathered over the course of her life.

Ali Smith lives in Cambridge.

Josephine Abbott, born in Manchester, studied Latin & English Language at Sheffield University and now lives in Derby. Has had poems published in magazines such as *Acumen*, *Agenda*, *The Frogmore Papers*, *Stand* and others, and has won prizes and commendations in a range of competitions, including Lancaster LitFest 2000, and The National Poetry Competition in 1999. First full collection is *Trying not to Levitate*, published by Blinking Eye.

Bobbie Allen, daughter of a nurse and a trucker, is a teacher in a comprehensive school. She has lived in Cardiff all her life except for a brief, unsuccessful stint in That London. Bobbie is a rabid Cardiff City supporter, she loves champagne and winning a small Bridport is a very good excuse to go and buy a bottle.

Cheryl Alu lives in Los Angeles where she is a television and screen writer. She has had short fiction published in the *Mississippi Review*, *Other Voices*, *The Barcelona Review* and *The Robert Olen Butler Prize Anthology*.

Liz Bassett was born in Northampton in 1973 and educated at Cambridge. Her poems have been published by *The Red Wheelbarrow*, *White Leaf Review*, *Agenda Broadsheet*, *The Guardian Poetry Workshop*, and in the anthologies *My Mother Threw Knives* (Second Light Publications), *Solitaire* (Templar Poetry) and *New Poets from Britain and America* (White Leaf Press). Her first pamphlet is forthcoming from Knucker Press. More details on her writing can be found at: www.word-happening.blogspot.com.

Anna Britten is a freelance journalist living in Bath. After reading modern languages at Oxford, she spent several years in London working for record companies and then for *Time Out* magazine. Her short fiction has been published in the Bloomsbury anthology of Asham Award finalists 'Is This What You Want?', online at Eclectica and Prick Of The Spindle, broadcast in BBC Radio 4's Afternoon Reading slot, and shortlisted for various other competitions, including Fish. She is also the author of a music industry career guide now in its third edition. She's currently polishing her first novel and looking for an agent.

Alan Buckley was originally from Merseyside. He moved to Oxford in the eighties to study English and has lived there ever since. Among other things, he has worked as a forklift truck driver, a psychotherapist, and a poet in residence at a prison. His first pamphlet *Shiver* (published by tall-lighthouse) was the Poetry Book Society pamphlet choice for summer 2009. He has recently received an Arts Council writer's grant, and is working towards a first collection.

Jenny Clarkson lives in Lincoln with her partner and her son, just up the road from daughter and grandchildren. She works part-time at the town's arts centre. She says she attended the university of life but missed a lot of the lectures. She has an allotment and dances the flamenco. She started writing short stories only in January, since when she has set herself what seems to her a punishing schedule of one a month. Her winning story is the first she has submitted. Has published poetry with *Fire*, *Obsessed with Pipework*, *Poetry New*, *Dreamcatcher*, *The Interpreter's House* and *The North*. She has had poems in the following small anthologies: *Tundra Gap* published by Dreamcatcher, *Spires and Steeples* published by Arts North Kesteven, along with *Words in the Wolds Anthology 2008* published by Dream Catcher Books.

Rhonda Collis was born in Oliver, BC, Canada and received her BA in English at the University of Western Ontario in London, Ontario. She wore many hats before she seriously settled into writing poetry and fiction, studying creative writing at the University of Victoria with poetry teachers, Patrick Lane and Lorna Crozier among others. Currently, she is completing her fourth year of a five-year optional residency Master's degree in Creative Writing with the University of British Columbia in Canada. Since 2006, she has had poetry and short fiction published in literary journals and is at work on her first novel. She lives in the small community of Cobble Hill, north of Victoria, BC, Canada with her husband and two daughters. Her short story 'Parada' was published in *Room Magazine*, Vancouver, and 'The Gospel Truth' in *On Spec*, Edmonton, Alberta. Her poetry, 'Overnight Train' appeared in *The Antigonish Review*, Antigonish; 'Journey Across the Pond' in *Vancouver Magazine*, Vancouver and 'Sudbury, 1972' in *Regreen* (Poetry Anthology).

Biographies

Clare Diprose lives in north-east Somerset, where she works as a feltmaker. She studied creative writing with the Open College of the Arts from 1995 to 2000. Her poem 'Mammoth's Teeth' won the Poetry Can competition in 1997, and *'Plums'* was commended in the 2008 Plough Prize. R*ocks full of stars*, which brought together her felt and poems as book-art, toured with the South West Textile Group's exhibition 'Bound/Unbound'. She is distracted by birds and islands, but shared poetry sessions in Wells give her deadlines and encouragement. Two poems, 'Catching the Light' and 'Red', were in *Island* autumn/winter 2005, published by Essence Press.

Zach Falcon was born and raised in Alaska. He is a graduate of Columbia, the University of Michigan Law School, and the Iowa Writers' Workshop. He currently lives in Iowa City, where he is working on a novel.

Lydia Fulleylove is currently completing an Arts Council-funded combined arts project, *Wild Places,* at HMP Albany, Isle of Wight. She has worked there as Writer in Residence from 2004 to 2009: a life-changing experience which has absorbed and sparked much of her creative energy. She has also led creative writing projects for a range of healthcare groups and for young people. She writes poetry, short stories, articles and creative writing materials, and is particularly interested in radio drama and, after a brilliant Arvon course, is now working on two radio plays. She received a Writer's Award from ACE in 2007 to work on a first poetry collection and a pamphlet is at present being considered by Happenstance Press. Websites: www.shorewomen.org and www.hightide-poets.org

Her poetry and short stories have been published in a range of literary magazines and anthologies including *Smiths Knoll, The Interpreter's House, Iota, Staple, Envoi and Re-writing the Map* (Vane Women Press). Winner of Isle of Wight *Faber/Ottakar* poetry competition and runner up in the national competition in 1998. Her short story for young people 'Rose Petal Message' recently won second prize in the Henley-on-Thames Museum of River and Rowing, *Wind in the Willows* competition, June 2009. Her literature-based literacy and creative writing materials were published for Nelson Thornes Primary Literacy in 1998.

Helen Geoghegan was born in Carlow, Ireland and studied English at Trinity College, Dublin. She has had stories published in a number of anthologies. One of seven siblings, she was, she says, privileged to grow up with a ferocious quality of communication. A particular detail of how siblings communicate unconsciously can get her onto the writing frequency, as can Tupperware, skin and most body parts. She has won prizes in the London Writers Competition and the Legend Award and was shortlisted for the Fish Prize and Asham Award.

Writing has helped her get the hang of herself.

Kate Hendry teaches English & Creative Writing at Barlinnie Prison in Glasgow and for the Open University. She lives in Ayrshire with her partner, two children, six hens and a duck. In 2007 she was awarded a Scottish Arts Council New Writer's Bursary to write a collection of linked short stories. 'Dont Say Anything' is one of them. Her short stories have been published in *Mslexia*, *New Writing Scotland* and *Harpers* amongst others.

Nicholas Hogg won the inaugural New Writing Ventures prize for fiction. His novel, *Show Me the Sky* – 'An assured and gripping début', BBC Radio 3 — is published by Canongate. His most recent work features in *Notes From the Underground*, *Riptide* and *Litro*, as well as winner of the 2009 'Editor's Choice' award in the Raymond Carver Short Story contest. Website: www.nicholashogg.com

Ben Holden was born in Basingstoke in 1976 and grew up in North Wales. He recently completed the MA in Creative and Life Writing at Goldsmiths, University of London and now lives in Devon.

Rhiannon Hooson recently returned to mid-Wales after a spell in Mongolia, and is currently finishing a PhD at Lancaster University. Her work has appeared in various poetry journals, and in 2008 she won an Eric Gregory Award for poets under 30.

Christopher Horton lives and works in London. His poems have been published (or are forthcoming) in various magazines including *Iota*, *Fuselit*, *Dream Catcher*, *Other Poetry*, *The Wolf*, *Magma*, *Poetry London*, *Ambit* and *Stand*, and in the anthologies *City Lighthouse* (Tall Lighthouse) and *City State: The New London Poetry* (Penned in the Margins). He is also a regular reviewer of poetry for magazines, blogs and websites. He organises and hosts/co-hosts for East Words and The Sampler, two new London poetry events. He was recently commended in the National Poetry Competition.

Dore Kiesselbach studied writing at Oberlin College and, as a U.S. Department of Education Javits Fellow, at the University of Iowa. He has published widely in American and Canadian magazines such as *FIELD, New Letters, Boulevard* and *Malahat Review*. His first collection has been runner up or finalist in several first and open-book competitions, including the National Poetry Series and the 2009 Agnes Lynch Starrett Prize. He lives in Minnesota. Some recent publications include 'Aubade', *American Life in Poetry*, 2009; 'Prayers Regarding the Making of Two Houses One', *Poetry East*, 2009; 'Windmill', *South Carolina Review*, 2009; 'Morgue', *New Orleans Review*, 2009 and 'Subjunctive', Barrow Street, 2008.

Joshua Lobb is Lecturer in Creative Writing at the University of Wollongong, Australia. He received his PhD from the University of New South Wales in 2004. Scholarly papers include: 'I could just walk out of this inconvenient story', 'Narrative Possibility in the Fairy Tales of A.S. Byatt' (UEA, 2009), 'Degrees of Relation: Iris Murdoch and A.S. Byatt' (ibidem-Verlag, 2009), and (with Dr Malcolm Ryan) '*The Tale of Peter Rabbit*: A Case Study in Story-Sense Reasoning' (AAAI, 2007). He is the writer of the plays *Daedalus, Wilde Tales* and *Still at Aulis*. He is currently working on a prose piece entitled *The Centre of It All*.

Nick MacKinnon teaches maths and English at Winchester College. He has had a few poems published in *Smiths Knoll*, *Warwick Review* and *Anon*. He has won some competitions but coming second in the Bridport is basically beginner's luck.

Annemarie Neary was educated in Dublin, at Trinity College and King's Inns. She joined the general exodus of the late eighties and moved to London to work as a lawyer. Eventually, after many years of joint-operating agreements, she succumbed to the charms of Venice, in the form of an MA in Venetian Renaissance art at the Courtauld Institute. Earlier this year, she won the Bryan MacMahon short story award at Listowel Writers' Week and came third in the Fish International Short Story award. She has written a novel, currently unpublished, set in neutral Ireland in

1941 and is in the midst of writing another, from which this story is taken. She is also working on a collection of short stories set in Venice. She lives in London with her husband and their three sons.

N Nye's widely published stories have appeared in *Glimmer Train*, *Cutthroat*, *Writers' Forum*, *bananafish*, *Inkwell*, *Open Windows 2006*, and an anthology, *Higher Elevations: Stories from the West*. 'Notes of the Oldest Daughter', a novel excerpt, was published by Writers' Forum, 1977. She lives in Longmont and Westcreek, Colorado, U.S.A.

Helen Oswald's pamphlet, *The Dark Skies Society*, was published by Waterloo Press. Her debut collection, *Learning Gravity*, is due from tall-lighthouse next spring. Helen's poems have appeared in a number of anthologies and poetry magazines, including *Magma*, *Poetry Review*, *The Rialto* and *Poetry London*. She currently works as an editor in Brighton. *The Dark Skies Society* was published by Waterloo Press (2004) and *Learning Gravity* is forthcoming from tall-lighthouse (2010).

Joanna Quinn was born in London, but grew up in Weymouth, Dorset, where she started her career as a journalist on the *Dorset Echo*. After living and working in Bristol for some years, she has returned to Dorset, this time to work in public relations. She is currently studying for an Mphil in Creative Writing at the University of Glamorgan and came second in the Bridport Prize last year. Joanna has also had a short story published in a Leaf Books anthology of the winners of their Open Short Story Competition 2006 and had a story featured in the *New Welsh Review*. She was recently chosen to be one of nine writers to be awarded a place on the Jerwood/Arvon Mentoring Scheme 2009 (http://www.arvonfoundation.org/p201.html) and is now working on her first novel.

Vidyan Ravinthiran was born in 1984 and is a graduate student and lecturer at Balliol College, Oxford. His pamphlet, *At Home or Nowhere*, was published by tall-lighthouse last year. Other poems have appeared in *Magma*, *Poetry Review*, *The North*, *The TLS* and are forthcoming in *Ambit* and *Stand*.

Natasha Soobramanien grew up in London, Hong Kong and Hastings. Natasha's writing has appeared in *Magnetic Promenade and other*

Sculpture Parks, edited by Chris Evans, and *New Writing 14*, edited by Lavinia Greenlaw and Helon Habila. She has recently contributed three chapters to Luke Williams' novel *The Echo Chamber* (Hamish Hamilton), which will be published in June 2010. Together with Luke Williams, Natasha co-organises Plum, an occasional live literature night: www.plumlive.co.uk She is a graduate of the MA in Creative Writing at UEA, and currently lives in Edinburgh, where she is working on a novel. She enjoys the company of dogs and poets. Website: www.plumlive.co.uk

Teresa Stenson's first novel was written by hand, each word in a different coloured crayon (it wasn't very long). She thinks her Mum might still have it somewhere. She started writing seriously (in black and white) four years ago and her short stories have been published widely, both in print and online, in places such as *Brand Literary Magazine, Writers' Forum,* and *The Orphan Leaf Review*. She lives in York where she works in a cinema and writes in coffee shops, trying not to look like she's listening to other people's conversations. She is working on a novel. You can read more about Teresa, her writing and her eavesdropping at www.teresa-stenson.blogspot.com.